Film & TV

ANIMAL STAR COLLECTIBLES

Film & TV
ANIMAL STAR
COLLECTIBLES

Dana Cain

ANTIQUE TRADER BOOKS

A Division of
Landmark Specialty Publications
Norfolk, Virginia

Dedication

This book is dedicated to Tippy, my first dog, a Shetland sheepdog/German shepherd mix. Although she was never famous, Tippy remains the greatest animal star of my childhood memory. She is the reason I love animals as much as I do.

ISBN: 0-930625-98-6

Library of Congress Catalog Card Number: 98-71060

Editor: Allan W. Miller

Copy Editor: Sandra Holcombe

Designer: Heather Ealey

Editorial Assistant: Wendy Chia-Klesch

Printed in the United States of America

To order additional copies of this book, or to obtain a catalog, please contact:

Antique Trader Books

P.O. Box 1050

Dubuque, Iowa 52004

or call 1-800-334-7165

Contents

Acknowledgments 8

Introduction 9

Rin Tin Tin 10

Lassie 20

Silver 42

Smokey Bear 54

Trigger 74

Flipper 86

Benji 100

Spuds MacKenzie 108

Babe 118

Wishbone 124

Disney's Animal Stars 134
    Barefoot Executive 136
    Big Red 136
    Cat from Outer Space, The 136
    Charlie the Lonesome Cougar 137
    Gordy 137
    Greyfriars Bobby 137
    Gus 137
    Horse in the Gray Flannel Suit, The 138
    Homeward Bound, The Incredible Journey 138
    Homeward Bound II: Lost in San Francisco 138
    Incredible Journey, The 139
    Iron Will 139
    King of the Grizzlies 139
    Legend of Lobo, The 139
    Littlest Outlaw, The 140
    $1,000,000 Duck 140
    Miracle of the White Stallions 140
    Monkey's Uncle, The 140
    Monkeys, Go Home! 141
    Napoleon and Samantha 141
    Nikki, Wild Dog of the North 141
    Old Yeller 141
    Operation Dumbo Drop 142
    Perri 142

Rascal 143
Ride a Wild Pony 143
Savage Sam 143
Shaggy Dog, The 143
Shaggy D.A., The 143
So Dear to My Heart 144
That Darn Cat 145
Three Lives of Thomasina, The 145
Tiger Walks, A 145
Toby Tyler, or Ten Weeks with the Circus 145
Tonka 146
Ugly Daschund, The 147
White Fang 147
White Fang 2: Myth of the White Wolf 147

Western Horse Stars 148
Black Eyed Nellie 149
Black Diamond 149
Black Jack 149
Buttermilk 150
Champion 151
Diablo 153
Fury 153
Gypsy 155
Koko 155
Silver 156
Snowfire 156
Target 157
Thunder the Wonder Horse 158
Tony 158
Topper 159
White Cloud 162
White Flash 162
Hartland Horse and Rider Sets 163

Menagerie 166
Asta 167
Beethoven 168
Ben (the bear) 169
Ben (the rat) 170
Black Beauty 170
Black Stallion 171
Bruce the Ocelot 172
Budweiser Clydesdales 172
Bullet 173
C.J. and other orangutans 174
Champy 175
Cheetah 175
Chinook the Wonder Dog 176
Clarence the Cross-Eyed Lion (and Daktari) 176
Cleo 177
Cujo 178

Daisy 178
Digby 178
Dobermans 179
Dog of Flanders 179
Dunston 179
Eddie 180
Elsa 180
Francis the Talking Mule 181
Fred 182
Frogs 183
Gentle Ben 183
J. Fred Muggs (and Mr. Kokomo) 184
Joe 185
Jonathan Livingston Seagull 185
Keiko (Free Willy) 186
King 188
Lad, A Dog 188
Lancelot Link, Secret Chimp 189
Leo, the MGM Lion 189
Marquis Chimps 190
Mister Ed 190
Misty of Chincoteague (and other Chincoteague Ponies) . . . 191
Morris 193
National Velvet (and International Velvet) 193
Nipper 194
Pete the Pup 195
Rex 195
Rusty 196
Skippy the Bush Kangaroo 196
Strongheart 197
Tamba the Talented Chimp 197
Toto 197
Vance the Talking Pig 198
White Fury 198
Willy 199
Yukon King 199
Zeus and Roxanne 199
Miscellaneous and Group Shots 199

The Patsy Award Winners 200

Acknowledgments

Animal Planet; Bethesda, Maryland
Atomic Antiques; Denver, Colorado
Jodi Bilsten; Fuji Photo Lab; Denver, Colorado
Carol and Donald Bretz; Arvada, Colorado; Smokey Bear collection
Lori Cain; New Orleans, Louisiana; Babe collection
Bruce Carteron; Denver, Colorado; movie posters and lobby cards
Kent Cordray; Denver, Colorado
Equity Toys; Los Angeles, California; Wishbone
Scott Gaeta; Denver, Colorado
Robert Klippel; Denver, Colorado
Sandy and Dennis Lanham; Longmont, Colorado; Spuds MacKenzie collection
Jan Lindenberger; Colorado Springs, Colorado
Scott Nelson; Denver, Colorado
Pat Roberts; Golden, Colorado; Trigger collection
Tod Stutzman; Clearwater, Florida; Flipper Chalkboard photograph
Universal Studios; Universal City, California; Babe material
Xeno Toys; Denver, Colorado

Introduction

Animals have a special way of touching the heart. Perhaps, because they act out of instinct and genuine caring, we know that when they show emotion, it is heartfelt, not fabricated. For centuries, people and animals have worked on building special bonds, on forging relationships built on special trust and caring.

These bonds have been portrayed, again and again, in film and television. Whether it's Rin Tin Tin howling and heartbroken over the loss of his master, or Flipper, swimming to the rescue of the boys he loves, we have been shown the incredible, enduring strength of the bond between man and animal.

And so, animal stars have come to mean a lot to us. They remind us about unconditional love and loyalty. Lassie, Old Yeller, Trigger, Benji, and Babe each shared a special bond with the humans in their lives. And so did many others.

Because many of us grew up with animal stars as primary childhood icons, they carry meaning into adulthood. And, when it occurs to us that we want to collect something, we often turn to things from our halcyon days of youth, things that remind us of where we came from, of who we are.

This is how some of us begin collecting animal stars. And, once the hobby has commenced, it rarely subsides. In fact, often a collector will start collecting, for instance, Trigger, then gradually add in other cowboy horses, such as Topper, Silver, Champion . . . or an Old Yeller collection will grow to include all Disney dog stars.

Collecting animal stars is fun and rewarding. Whether your particular favorite has an important message ("Remember—Only You Can Prevent Forest Fires") or whether you take a more lighthearted approach (Are you listening, Spuds MacKenzie collectors?) it's a pastime that can offer years of happy hunting and unexpected discoveries.

Rin Tin Tin

Fire, smoke, gunshots! The scene is set against an important World War I battle. Americans and Germans are fighting for control of a German airfield, and a downed plane is burning near the dugout in northern France. American soldiers notice, inside the burning plane, a German shepherd dog is howling beside its dead master.

No, this isn't a scene from one of Rin Tin Tin's films. It's a scene from his life. Two days later, on a cold September day, the German shepherd rescued from the plane gives birth to five puppies. Two of them, bright-eyed but undernourished brother and sister, are adopted by Sgt. Lee Duncan, a pilot from California. Duncan and his platoon nurse the pair back to health, feeding them condensed milk.

The pups are named Rin Tin Tin and Nanette, after small, woolen good luck dolls French girls gave soldiers returning to the front lines. The names originated from a French legend . . . During the early days of World War I, when Paris was being shelled by Germans, about 40 people took refuge in an underground railway station. It was bombed, and everyone died except a French girl, Nanette, and her sweetheart, Rin Tin Tin. Soon, people believed the names brought good luck, and girls began to knit fluffy woolen dolls, calling them Rin Tin Tin and Nanette. The puppies, soft and helpless, just a few days old, reminded Duncan of those fluffy little dolls.

Rin Tin Tin soon became the platoon mascot, accompanying Duncan on dangerous missions and running medical supplies from camp to camp. He grew up in a war zone, and seemed comfortable even in the most deadly environments, showing bravery few could match.

Rin Tin Tin flew on 36 flights with Duncan, all involving combat. On one harrowing mission, Rin Tin Tin and Sgt. Duncan were under enemy fire for more than four hours.

At last, when the war was over, Duncan was scheduled to return to California. Although Customs prohibited him from taking Rin Tin Tin and Nanette home, Duncan fought and negotiated until permission was granted, and he and the dogs left the war zone, and flew to Duncan's sheep farm in sunny California.

But Rin Tin Tin was not destined to spend the rest of his life calmly tending sheep. Not quite. Duncan realized that his dog had a special star quality—a mix of intelligence, bravery, and team spirit that would make for an excellent career in Hollywood.

Rin Tin Tin's first film was *The Man from Hell's River* (1922). It launched the dog into an incredible career, starring in a very successful string of silent movies and serials. Rin Tin Tin managed an effortless move into "talkies," ("barkies" as far as he was concerned) and he worked until 1931. Between 1922 and 1931, he starred in 28 films. Rin Tin Tin was the ultimate macho dog star. A German shepherd to be reckoned with, he was all action—with the bark and the bite to back it up. Duncan managed to teach Rin Tin Tin an estimated 500 commands. At the height of his popularity, Rin Tin Tin received 10,000-20,000 fan letters a week. He saved Warner Brothers from bankruptcy, providing the studio with its primary source of income for several years.

According to an old issue of *Collier's*, when not on the film set, Rin Tin Tin lived in luxury—a kennel designed like a "Stucco miniature palace, fitted with electric lights, artistic ventilators, running water, and a silver food trough—even a radio set, fans and electric heating apparatus!"

Rin Tin Tin died on August 10, 1932, at age 14, while working on a film called *Pride of the Legion*. He had been romping with Lee Duncan in their front yard, when the dog jumped into Duncan's arms and went completely limp. As Duncan fell to the ground, cradling the dog, neighbor Jean Harlow ran over to see what was wrong. They both cradled Rin Tin Tin in their arms, crying as the beloved dog's spirit left his body.

But, Rin Tin Tin's legacy did not die with him. During his lifetime, Rin Tin Tin had sired no less than 48 puppies. One of them, dubbed Rin Tin Tin Jr., exhibited some of his father's show biz pizzazz, and took over in his father's paw steps. His mother, Champion Asta of Linwood, also owned by Lee Duncan, was valued at $3,500 in 1936.

Rin Tin Tin Jr., called "Rinty," zoomed through doggie kindergarten with flying colors, and was so well educated by 11 months that he was put under contract and worked consistently for the rest of his life. Rinty starred in several movies during the 1930s, including *The Wolf Dog* (1933 serial). He also starred in a few projects with Rex, King of the Wild Horses, including *The Adventures of Rex and Rinty* (1935 serial), and *The Law of the Wild*.

Rinty also took over the title role in his father's radio show. *Rin Tin Tin* was first broadcast over NBC Blue in 1930. Ken-L-Ration sponsored the show, which ran until 1934 (sponsored by CBS its final year.)

In 1954, Rinty's pup, again named Rin Tin Tin, carried his grandfather's legacy to television. *Rin Tin Tin*, the TV series, made its debut on ABC on October 15, 1954, starring Rin Tin Tin as a heroic German shepherd living at a cavalry fort in the 1880s. In this series, Rin Tin Tin and his companion, Rusty (Lee Aaker), a young boy, were the only survivors of an Indian raid on a wagon train. They were taken to Fort Apache to live, and promptly assigned the ranks of private and corporal, respectively.

Alongside human companions Rip Masters (Jim L. Brown) and young Rusty, Rin Tin Tin helped fight off Indians and other bad guys for four seasons (164 episodes).

Following the initial success of the television series, another radio show was introduced in 1955. This one, sponsored by Milk Bone, followed the adventures of Rinty and Rusty on the American Frontier.

During the 1960s and 1970s, Rin Tin Tin's popularity waned as Lassie's more feminine, nurturing approach won the hearts of America's viewers. But, Rin Tin Tin was not forgotten, and in 1988, he resurfaced in the Canadian CBN production of *Rin Tin Tin, K-9 Cop*.

Over the decades, an incredible array of Rin Tin Tin collectibles have been produced, including plush toys, plastic figures, playsets, View-Master packets, books, comics, coloring books, movie posters, lobby cards, and more.

Rin Tin Tin Partial Filmography

1922—*The Man from Hell's River*
1923—*Where the North Begins*
1924—*Find Your Man*
1926—*The Night Cry*
1927—*Dog of the Regiment*
1927—*Jaws of Steel*
1928—*Rinty of the Desert*
1929—*Frozen River*
1929—*Tiger Rose*
1930—*The Lone Defender* (serial)
1930—*Rough Waters*
1931—*The Lightning Warrior*
1932—*Pride of the Legion*

Rin Tin Tin Jr. ("Rinty")

1933—*The Wolf Dog* (serial, 12 chapters)
1935—*The Adventures of Rex and Rinty*
(serial, with Rex, King of the Wild Horses)
1947—*The Return of Rin Tin Tin*

Rin Tin Tin Collectibles Price Guide

Figure 1-1

Banner, Fighting Blue Devils, 101st Cavalry,
8.5 in., blue felt, Nabisco premium $20-30

Beanie, premium 40-65

Book, *The Story of Rin Tin Tin*, biography and
picture book, Whitman, 1927 *(figure 1-1)* 30-50

Book, *Rin Tin Tin and the Lost Indian*, Little Golden
Book 276, photo cover, 1956 *(figure 1-2)* 10-15

Book, *Rin Tin Tin and the Outlaw*, Little Golden
Book 304, photo cover, 1957 *(figure 1-3)* 10-15

Book, *Rin Tin Tin and Rusty*, Little Golden
Book 246, 1955 (*figure 1-4*) $10-15

Book, *Rin Tin Tin—One of the Family*, 8.25 x
7.5 in., Whitman Cozy Corner Book, 1953 10-15

Book, *Rin Tin Tin's Rinty*, Whitman TV hardcover,
photo cover, 1954 (*figure 1-5*) 12-18

Book, *Rin Tin Tin and Call to Danger*, Whitman
TV hardcover, 1957 (*figure 1-6*) 12-18

Book, *Rin Tin Tin and the Ghost Wagon Train*,
Whitman TV hardcover, 1958 (*figure 1-7*) 12-18

Book, *Rinty and Pals for Rusty*, Whitman Tell-a-Tale
Book, 1957 10-15

Book, *Rin Tin Tin and the Hidden Treasure*, Big
Golden Book, 1958 12-20

Book, *The Rin Tin Tin Book of Dog Care*, by Lee
Duncan, 1958 25-35

Canteen, Official Rin Tin Tin 101st Cavalry, brown
plastic with strap, 7 in., Nabisco premium 18-25

Chalkware Figure, 11 in., rhinestone eyes,
name on base, 1930s 60-90

Coloring Book, *Adventures of Rin Tin Tin*, with
cake photo on cover, Whitman, 1955 15-25

Coloring Book, *Adventures of Rin Tin Tin*, with
Rusty and girl on balcony, Whitman, 1957 15-25

Figure 1-2

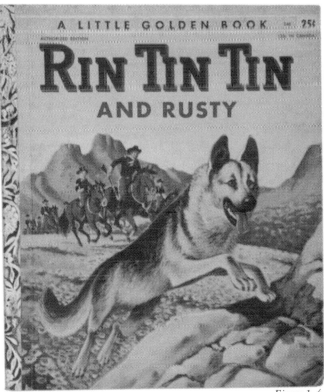

Figure 1-4

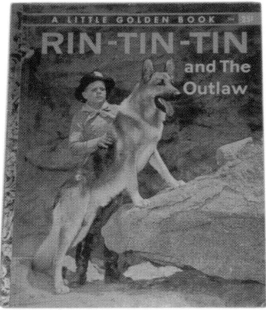

Figure 1-3

Figure 1-7

Coloring Fun Set, crayons, pictures to color, slates, 20 x 14 in. box, Transogram, 1956 . . . . $85-135

Comic Book Series, Rin Tin Tin, Dell Publishing 1952-1961
    #1 *Rin Tin Tin in Dark Danger* (Dell Four Color 434), 1952 30-130

    #2 (Dell Four Color #476) 10-70

    #3 (Dell Four Color #523) 10-70

    #4-20 *(figure 1-8 a-d)* 10-50

    #21-38 10-40

Comic Book, *Rin Tin Tin & Rusty* #1, Gold Key, November, 1963 10-50

Comic Book, *Calling All Boys* #11, May, 1947, photo on cover and inside story 10-20

Comic Book, *Rin Tin Tin*, March of Comics, 5 x 7 in., store premium, 1957, photo cover 15-30

Costume, Rin Tin Tin, brown and black, with picture on chest and plastic mask, 1956 75-95

Costume, Rusty, with Rin Tin Tin pictured, plastic mask, Ben Cooper, 1950s 60-90

Costume Hat, Fighting Blue Devils 101 Cavalry, blue felt, Nabisco premium, 1950s 40-50

Costume Mask, Rusty 101 Cavalry, 9 in., plastic, Nabisco premium, 1950s 20-30

Cup, "Yo Ho Rinty/Rin Tin Tin and Rusty," yellow
plastic, 3 in., Nabisco premium, 1954-1956 .. $45-75

Dog Food Box, Ken-L-Biskit, Rin Tin Tin on
4 x 4 in. box, Chappel Bros., 1932 25-35

Figure, painted hard plastic, 6.5 in. tall, photo
tag reads "Fighting Blue Devils," late 1950s 65-80

Game, "The Adventures of Rin Tin Tin,"
Transogram, 1955 60-90

Game, bead-in-the-hole type, 1.5 in., Nabisco
premium came in cereal box, 1950s 12-20

Gun, metal and plastic pistol with black leather
holster, Nabisco premium, 1950s 100-150

Lobby Card, *Find Your Man* (scene dependent) 25-75

Lobby Card, *Hills of Kentucky* (scene dependent) . . . 25-75

Magic Erasable Pictures, boxed set with crayons,
sharpener, etc., Transogram, 1956 65-100

Matchbox, color, Rin Tin Tin graphic, Spanish
writing on bottom, 2.5 in., 1930s 25-35

Magazine, *Children's Playmate*, Rin Tin Tin
and Rusty cover, January 1958 25-35

Magazine, *Jack and Jill*, Rin Tin Tin cover,
July 1960 12-20

Figure 1-5

Figure 1-8a

Figure 1-6

Figure 1-8b

Movie Poster, *Adventures of Rex and Rinty,* with Rex, King of the Wild Horses, Mascot serial, 1935 . . . . $200-275

Movie Poster, *Find Your Man,* 1924 400-600

Movie Poster, *Hills of Kentucky* 400-600

Movie Poster, *The Lightning Warrior,* serial, 1931 175-225

Movie Poster, *The Lone Defender,* serial, 1930 serial 120-200

Movie Poster, *The Man from Hell's River,* Rin Tin Tin's first film, 1922 300-400

Movie Poster, *The Night Cry,* 1926 600-750

Movie Poster, *The Return of Rin Tin Tin,* 1947, Romay 50-750

Movie Poster, *Rinty of the Desert,* 1928 300-400

Movie Poster, *Rough Waters,* 1930 200-300

Movie Poster, *The Wolf Dog,* Mascot serial, 12 chapters, 1933 120-200

Notebook Binder, "Yo Ho Rinty" illustration on vinyl, 1957 30-40

Paint-by-Number Set, Transogram, 1950s 50-75

Pen, Rin Tin Tin Rifle Pen, 5 in., Nabisco
premium, with Nabisco mailing box $20-40

Photograph, B&W, 8 x 10 in., with printed
autographs of cast, Nabisco premium, 1955 20-30

Photograph, B&W, 8 x 10 in., Rin Tin Tin with
Al Jolson, studio PR shot, early 1930s 20-30

Pin-Back Button, head photo with name on
bottom, from Nabisco contest 12-20

Pin-Back Button, "Rin Tin Tin—The Lone
Defender," 1930s, B&W 15-25

Pin-Back Button, "Rin Tin Tin—The Lone
Defender," profile in circle, yellow, 1930s 10-15

Pin-Back Button, "I'm a Rin Tin Tin Booster/See
the Lone Defender . . . ," brown, 1930s 25-50

Pin-Back Button, "King of the Canines," B&W,
1930s 15-25

Pin-Back Button, "Rin Tin Tin Fan Club—A
Warner Bros. Star," 1930s 15-25

Pin-Back Button, "Rin Tin Tin in The Lightning
Warrior," 1930s 15-25

Pin-Back Button, head shot, no text, metal litho,
brown and white, 1930s 5-10

Playset, Rin Tin Tin at Fort Apache, Series 5000,
Marx #3658, 1956 (figure 1-9) 250-450

Figure 1-8d

Figure 1-8c

Playset, Rin Tin Tin at Fort Apache, Series 500,
    Marx #3628, 1956 . . . . $300-500

Playset, Rin Tin Tin at Fort Apache, Series 1000,
    Marx, 1956 200-300

Plush Toy, name on plastic collar, 11 in. long,
    rubber head, Smile Novelty, 1959 75-100

Plush Toy, plastic face, 36 in. long, My Toy,
    1965 40-75

Pocketknife, Rusty and Rin Tin Tin, morse
    code on back, 3.5 in., mid-1950s 45-65

Puzzle, jigsaw, boxed, Rusty and Rinty photo
    with sky, 63 pieces, Whitman 15-25

Puzzle, frame tray, Rinty and Rusty with
    camel, 14.5 in., Whitman, 1950s 15-25

Record Album, *Adventures of Rin Tin Tin*,
    33 1/3 rpm, TV cast, photo cover, Columbia 15-25

Record Album, *Rinty Breaks Through*,
    78 rpm, TV cast, Columbia, 1955 15-25

Record Album, *Adventures of Rin Tin Tin*,
    33 1/3 rpm, TV cast, Columbia, 1955 20-30

Record, "Forward Ho!" sung by Lt. Rip Masters,
    45 rpm, MGM, 1950s 20-30

Rings, Nabisco cereal premium, series of 12
    Rin Tin Tin rings, mid-1950s, each 50-65

Figure 1-9

Sign, "Rin Tin Tin Dog Supply Center," lithographed tin, 20 in. long, store display, 1956 . . . $65-95

Slate, Rin Tin Tin Magic Slate, with erasable
film cover, mid-1950s 20-30

Stereo Viewer, 4 in. wide, plastic, Nabisco
premium 20-35

Stereo View Picture Cards, 24 issued for viewer,
2 x 4 in., Nabisco premium, each 2-4

Stickers, Nabisco cereal prizes, 2.5 x 2.5 in.,
set of seven issued, 1958, each 8-12

Tie, child size, with printed Rusty autograph
and Rinty pawtograph, 1950s 40-60

Totem Pole, Nabisco cereal box punch-outs,
embossed 5 in. color cards, set of 8, each 8-12

Trading Card, Rin Tin Tin with monkey,
arcade card from late 1920s 4-7

TV Guide, cover story, Rin Tin Tin and Rusty
with Lassie and Timmy, July 2, 1955 30-40

TV Guide, "TV Animals—Better Off
Than Actors?" February 8-14, 1958 5-10

View-Master Set, "Rin Tin Tin," 3 reels with
package, Sawyer's, 1955 *(figure 1-10)* 15-25

Figure 1-10

Lassie

"I think Lassie's trying to tell us something."
— Hugh Reilly

For decades, America's favorite collie has delivered a message. With her distinctive bark, her compassionate whimper, and the gentle wag of her tail, she showed the baby boomer generation the meaning of love and loyalty. During the 17 years that Lassie starred on CBS (1954-1970), she consistently held the number one spot during her time slot. Lassie was a Sunday evening staple, as reliable and faithful as only man's best friend can be. The champion of many causes—including ecology, U.S. Savings Bonds, forestry and Campbell's Soup—Lassie was a baby boomer icon—and the dog we all wanted; the dog by which we measured our own dogs, be they purebreds or mutts. Lassie was the perfect pet.

Lassie was actually introduced in a 1938 *Saturday Evening Post* short story, "Lassie Come-Home," by Eric Knight. Two years later, Knight expanded the short story into a successful novel, which was picked up by MGM and produced for the silver screen. The 1943 box office hit starred Roddy McDowell and Pal, the first Lassie.

Pal went on to star in all seven of the MGM *Lassie* movies, and, 11 years after his first feature film, appeared in the *Lassie* television pilot, at age 14. Not bad for a dog who was introduced to his Hollywood trainer because he had an incurable lust for car chasing (which he never conquered).

Since then, eight of Pal's descendants (all male) have played Lassie. The most devoted fans and collectors can identify the different canine actors by sight, although they all share the trademark brown and white markings, fluffy white ruff, and white blaze down the nose. Howard, who starred in the 1994 *Lassie* film, and in the newest *Lassie* TV show, on Animal Planet, is currently carrying on the tradition of his great-great-great-great-great-grandfather. His trainer, Robert Weatherwax, is the son of Rudd Weatherwax, who owned and trained Pal and all the other Lassies.

Although she has been a household name for more than 50 years, Lassie's success has boomed and waned along the way. During the 1940s, the collie was one of MGM's most bankable movie stars. She worked with co-stars like Elizabeth Taylor, Peter Lawford, Jeanette MacDonald, Janet Leigh, and others. In 1947, Lassie starred in her own radio show, and by the time she hit the television airwaves in 1954, she was a phenomenon.

Lassie's television ratings were impressive for two decades, as she was transferred from Jeff Miller (Tommy Rettig) to Timmy Martin (Jon Provost) to Ranger Corey Stuart (Robert Bray). While living with Jeff and, later, Timmy, Lassie mastered the art of farm and family management. She showed the American TV-viewing public what the perfect pet should be like. She was a loyal, fastidious nanny to the boys, a farm hand for dad, and an invaluable helpmate for mom. She helped solve simple rural mysteries (Are spacemen stealing Ruth's bananas?), made friends with the neighbor dogs (like Pokey, the basset hound), served as a juvenile crime stopper (Which of Timmy's classmates stole the Lone Ranger Peace Patrol money?), and was credited with many a daring rescue mission.

Only once did she falter in an assignment. Ruth Martin (June Lockhart) had stepped into a bear trap, and instructed Lassie to run home and bring back a C-Clamp. The dutiful dog raced home and, as the helpless Ruth was about to be eaten by a mountain lion, Lassie returned in the nick of time . . . with a cheese slicer.

Of course, Lassie managed to correct the error, and, of course, Lassie saved Ruth. So, she was forgiven. After all, the two items *do* look pretty similar, especially to someone who's never been to home economics or shop class.

When Lassie took up residence with a forest ranger ten years after her television debut, her responsibilities increased. The collie's range of influence broadened, and she found herself overseeing an entire landscape full of lost children, wounded campers, frightened fauna, and unpredictable predators. These were action-packed episodes, which helped move Lassie into a position as one of the nation's strongest environmental advocates. Unfortunately, while Lassie was battling litter and pollution, her co-star, Robert Bray, was battling alcoholism off-camera. By 1968, CBS was forced to replace him with two new rangers (played by Jed Allan and Jack De Mave).

In 1971, when television's prime time parameters were changed, CBS made the inexplicable decision to cancel *Lassie*. Shocked, but determined to continue the legacy, Lassie's owner/trainer, Rudd Weatherwax, took control, rounded-up advertising support, and created a syndicated Lassie show which aired during its old, familiar time slot in many cities. This time, Lassie was teamed with the Holden family, which included several children—boys and girls. Unfortunately, however, the magic just wasn't there. The series ceased production in 1974.

During that same time, an animated Lassie was born. *Lassie's Rescue Rangers* aired on Saturday mornings between 1973-1975, and marked the collie's return to forestry. It, however, lacked the staying power of the original TV show. In 1978, another attempt to revive Lassie met with lukewarm response. An enjoyable feature film, *The Magic of Lassie*, co-starred Jimmy Stewart and Mickey Rooney.

What followed was a Lassie-less decade. For the first time since the early 1940s, there were no new Lassie adventures. The American population became infatuated with a new yuppie lifestyle, and seemed too busy jogging and building their portfolios to appreciate Lassie's simple life lessons.

Finally, in 1989, the syndicated *New Lassie*, series was born, starring Christopher and Dee Wallace Stone as the loving parents of two great kids (Wendy Cox and Will Nipper). The series, which, until recently aired on the Family Channel, captured the old Lassie spirit, if not the old ratings. Jon Provost was a series regular as Uncle Steve, and June Lockhart made a tear-jerking guest appearance as Ruth Martin. Tom Rettig appeared on the show as well. And, in an ongoing tribute, the *New Lassie* featured several episodes with Roddy McDowell as children's author A. W. Leeds. There was no doubt that this was really Lassie, and the show's creators understood and loved the dog's legacy.

Unfortunately, decent ratings eluded that *Lassie* series, as well as the 1994 *Lassie* feature film. Film critic Roger Ebert approved of the movie, however, noting, "One of the joys of Lassie is the way she so patiently and cleverly manages the lives of the humans that God has given her . . . It's reassuring these days, to see a movie where there's no problem Lassie can't solve."

Lassie's newest venture, a series on Animal Planet, has her once again paired with a young boy named Timmy. The series takes viewers to Hudson Falls, Vermont, where the recently widowed veterinarian Karen Cabot has moved with her son, Timmy. Separated from his friends, Timmy finds a new companion in a certain collie that he meets in a local junkyard. Together, Timmy and Lassie make new friends and lead them on a series of exciting adventures.

Lassie collectors are a special breed. They don't mind that there's some 50 years of memorabilia to track down. They seem undaunted by the scarcity and price tags associated with some of the rarer pieces. If that dog is on it, they have to have it.

The earliest Lassie collectible is the *Saturday Evening Post* dated December 17, 1938, which featured Eric Knight's original short story, "Lassie Come-Home." For many, however, the printed Lassie isn't as desirable as the Lassie of film and television.

With the release of the movie *Lassie Come Home* (MGM dropped the hyphen), and the subsequent MGM *Lassie* movies in the 1940s and early 1950s, Lassie memorabilia was born. Movie posters, promotional stills, press kits, and lobby cards from Lassie's early films are among her more valuable collectibles today. A lobby card from *Lassie Come Home* which shows the dog (most did not), sells for about $40. The one-sheet easily brings $200. Memorabilia from *The Courage of Lassie* is also very high-priced, due to the cross-over collectibility of Lassie's co-star, Elizabeth Taylor.

As the collie's fame grew, so did the demand for Lassie souvenirs. By the time she had entrenched herself as a Sunday night television favorite in the 1950s, a wealth of merchandise was available.

Among the most memorable pieces is a board game, The Adventures of Lassie, released in 1955 by Lisbeth Whiting. The colorful game features barking "bow wow" buttons; Lassie pawns showing the collie in red, yellow, blue, and green; and squares labeled "fights alligator," "brings note," "hurts paw," "finds treasure," etc. (A later board game, released by Game Gems in 1965, is cursed with one of the worst artistic renderings of Lassie ever created.)

Also in the 1950s, the Breyer Molding Co., famous for its highly collectible line of plastic horses, issued an unmarked Lassie figure. The white plastic collie, spray-painted brown with a bright-red tongue, is hard to find today.

Lassie inflatables from the 1950s, including a wading pool, a beach ball, and a swim ring, are quite rare today. Another oddity, a Lassie Halloween costume issued by Collegeville in 1956, is also near the top of every Lassie collector's list.

In the late 1950s, Campbell's offered a Lassie wallet through the mail, while Swanson sponsored a Lassie Friendship Ring promotion. The ring, which could be had for "25 cents and a label from Swanson meat pies or TV brand dinners" in 1957, now fetches considerably more, for anyone lucky enough to find one. Lassie also loaned her image to Red Heart Dog Food (which produced a very collectible comic book featuring the collie in 1949), and more recently to Recipe Brand Dog food (1969) and Ken-L Ration's Gravy Train (1994).

Dell comics also jumped on the Lassie bandwagon, issuing more than 60 Lassie comic books between 1950 and 1967. The company's title, "M-G-M's Lassie" featured beautiful painted covers before switching to photo covers and simplifying the title to "Lassie" in 1957 (issue #37). Dell became Gold Key in January 1963, and the company's last Lassie comic (#69) was published in 1967. Issue number one is the only M-G-M issue to feature a photo cover.

Lassie was also featured in the smaller-sized March of Comics line, given away as promotions for various stores. That line included 11 Lassie comics between 1959 and 1976.

In 1966, Gold Key Lassie comics sponsored a special mail-order offer allowing boys and girls to become Lassie Forest Rangers for a $1 membership fee. The official Lassie Forest Ranger Kit included color photos of Lassie and Ranger Corey Stuart, an official Lassie Forest Ranger badge and iron-on emblem, a handbook touting the benefits of the U.S. Forest Service, and an official vinyl wallet containing an official Lassie Forest Ranger I.D. card, insignia, picture of Lassie, and membership card.

Lassie has been the subject of loads of books, coloring books, and magazine features over the years. Whitman, alone, has produced dozens of books, coloring books and puzzles. That company's line of hardcover "Authorized TV Edition" books, published between the late 1950s and early 1970s, features more Lassie titles than any other TV show title.

One of the better finds in the Lassie coloring book category is a boxed set of 12 books that Whitman issued in the late 1950s, complete with eight crayons.

Although some Lassie collectors would rather dismiss the animated Lassie's *Rescue Rangers* series, original animation cels from the Saturday morning show are now worth hundreds of dollars. No Lassie collection can be truly complete without one.

Since Lassie is an animal star, it stands to reason that a variety of stuffed animal toys have been produced over the years. Knickerbocker, Gund, and Dakin have all issued stuffed Lassies, most reclining, in varying sizes. In 1990, Gund released a limited edition series of plush Lassies in various sizes and poses.

Also on the list of rare-but-recent Lassie collectibles are items produced and sold exclusively at the Dog Museum in St. Louis to commemorate Lassie's 50th Anniversary in 1993. The museum published a magazine-style booklet called *Lassie: A Collie and Her Influence* which includes an article on Lassie collectibles, and features some wonderful photographs of rare Lassie memorabilia. The museum also issued a Warhol-style Lassie T-shirt celebrating the anniversary. Both pieces are now out of print.

Lassie Filmography

1943—*Lassie Come Home* (Roddy McDowell)

1945—*Son of Lassie* (Peter Lawford)

1946—*Courage of Lassie* (Elizabeth Taylor)

1948—*Hills of Home* (Edmund Gwenn, Janet Leigh)

1949—*The Sun Comes Up* (Jeanette MacDonald)

1950—*Challenge to Lassie* (Edmund Gwenn, Donald Crisp, Alan Napier)

1951—*The Painted Hills* (Paul Kelly—last MGM *Lassie* movie)

1963—*Lassie's Great Adventure* (Jon Provost, Hugh Reilly, June Lockhart—Theatrically released version of 5-part television episode, *The Journey*)

1978—*The Magic of Lassie* (James Stewart, Mickey Rooney)

1994—*Lassie* (Thomas Guiry, Helen Slater)

Lassie on Television

1954-57—*Lassie*, CBS (Tom Rettig as Jeff Miller)

1958-64—*Lassie*, CBS (Jon Provost as Timmy Martin)

1964-68—*Lassie*, CBS (Robert Bray as Ranger Corey Stuart)

1968-71—*Lassie*, CBS (Jed Allan and Jack De Mave as rangers)

1971-74—*Lassie*, syndicated (The Holden family)

1973-75—*Lassie's Rescue Rangers* (animated Saturday morning series)

1989-91—*The New Lassie*, syndicated (Christopher and Dee Wallace Stone, Jon Provost as Uncle Steve)

1997-present—*Lassie*, Animal Planet/Discovery Channel

Lassie Collectibles Price Guide

Advertisement, Lassie with radio mike for
Red Heart Dog Food, *Saturday Evening Post*,
1940s *(figure 2-1)* $5-10

Animation Cel, Lassie's Rescue Rangers,
Filmation, framed (1973) 350-400

Autograph, Jon Provost *(figure 2-2)* 25-35

Autograph, June Lockhart 30-45

Bend-Ems, 1994, sitting or standing pose,
JusToys, carded 5-10

Board Game, "Adventures of Lassie," 1955,
Lisbeth Whiting *(figure 2-3)* 65-75

Board Game, "Lassie," 1965, Game Gems
(figure 2-4) 20-25

Book, *Adventures in Alaska*, Whitman Big Little
Book, 1967, hard or soft cover, color interior
(figure 2-5a) 10-12

Book, *The Adventures of Lassie*, Giant Little Golden
Book, three stories, 1958 *(figure 2-6)* 12-15

Book, *The Busy Morning*, Whitman Tell-a-Tale Book,
1973 *(figure 2-7)* 5-8

Book, *Challenge to Lassie*, film book with color plates,
80 illustrations, Ward, Lock & Co., England,
1950 50-65

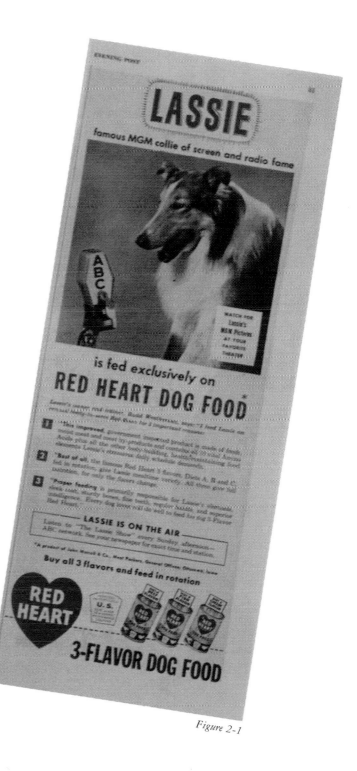

Figure 2-1

Figure 2-2

Figure 2-4

Figure 2-7

Book, *Forbidden Valley*, photo cover with Timmy, Whitman, 1959 . . . . $10-15

Book, *Hooray for Lassie!* Whitman Tell-a-Tale Book, 1964 5-8

Book, *Lassie*, by Sheila Black, soft cover movie novelization with photos, 7.75 x 5 in., Puffin, 1994 2-4

Book, *Lassie: A Collie and Her Influence*, 1993, published by the Dog Museum *(figure 2-8)* 10-20

Book, *Lassie and Her Day in the Sun*, photo cover, Golden Book, 1958 *(figure 2-9)* 8-12

Book, *Lassie and Her Friends*, soft cover, Golden Shape Book, 1975 5-8

Book, *Lassie and the Big Clean-Up Day*, Golden Book, 1971 6-10

Book, *Lassie and the Deer Mystery*, Whitman BIG Tell-a-Tale Book, 1966 *(figure 2-10a)* 6-10

Book, *Lassie and the Kittens*, Whitman Tell-a-Tale Book, 1956 *(figure 2-10b)* 10-15

Book, *Lassie and the Little Lost Sheep*, pop-up counting book, Seafarer, 1994 *(figure 2-11a)* 4-10

Book, *Lassie and the Lost Explorer*, Golden Book, 1958 *(figure 2-11b)* 8-12

Book, *Lassie and the Mystery of Blackberry Bog*, with dust jacket, Whitman, 1956 22-28

Book, *Lassie and the Mystery of Blackberry Bog*,
    bike cover, Whitman, 1956 . . . .$10-15

Book, *Lassie and the Mystery of Blackberry Bog*,
    swamp cover, Whitman, 1956 8-12

Book, *Lassie and the Secret Friend*, Big Golden
    Book, 1972 6-10

Book, *Lassie and the Secret of Summer*, art cover,
    Whitman, 1958 10-15

Book, *Lassie and the Secret of Summer*, photo cover,
    Whitman, 1958 10-15

Book, *Lassie and the Shabby Sheik*, red hard cover,
    color interior, Whitman Big Little Book, 1968
    (figure 2-5b) 10-15

Book, *Lassie and the Shabby Sheik*, blue soft cover,
    B&W interior, Whitman Big Little Book, 1968 . . 6-10

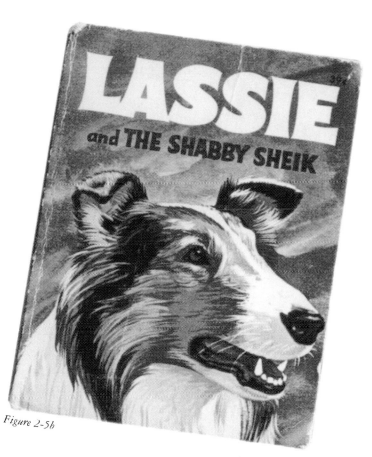

Figure 2-5b

Figure 2-6

Figure 2-5a

Figure 2-9

Figure 2-10a

Book, *Lassie's Brave Adventure*, Whitman Tell-a-Tale
Book, 1958 . . . . $8-12

Book, *Lassie Come-Home*, by Eric Knight, 1940
(most common editions, not 1st edition) 5-15

Book, *Lassie Come-Home*, Wonder Books adaptation,
1956 6-10

Book, *Lassie en un Rescate Peligroso*, Little Golden
Book, Spanish edition, soft cover, no. 61 8-15

Book, *Lassie Finds a Friend*, Whitman Tell-a-Tale
Book, 1960 6-10

Book, *Lassie Finds a Way*, Big Golden Book,
1957 12-15

Book, *The Lassie Method*, by Rudd Weatherwax,
1971 20-25

Figure 2-12

Book, *Lassie Shows the Way*, Golden Book, 1956 .. $10-15

Book, *Lost in the Snow*, Whitman, 1969 6-10

Book, *The Magic of Lassie*, Bantam, 1978, paperback movie novelization 5-8

Book, *The Mystery of Bristlecone Pine*, Whitman, 1968 6-10

Book, *Old One-Eye*, soft cover, B&W interior, Whitman Big Little Book, 1975, ... 6-10

Book, *Rescue in the Storm*, Cozy Corner Books, 1951 10-15

Book, *The Sandbar Rescue*, Whitman Tip Top Tale Book, 1964 10-15

Book, *The Secret of Smelter's Cave*, Whitman, 1968 .. 6-10

Figure 2-13

Figure 2-10b

Figure 2-11a

Figure 2-8

Book, *The Story of Lassie*, by John Rothwell and
Rudd Weatherwax, 1950 . . . .$35-45

Book, *The Sun Comes Up*, film book with color plates,
80 illustrations, Ward, Lock & Co., England,
1949 50-65

Book, *Treasure Hunter*, Whitman, 1960 10-15

Book, *The Wild Mountain Trail*, Ranger Corey
photo on back, Whitman, 1966 8-12

Coloring Book, Timmy and Lassie on cover,
Whitman, 1958 20-30

Coloring Book, black lamb on cover, Whitman,
1960 *(figure 2-12)* 12-18

Coloring Book, Ranger Corey on cover, Western
Publishing Co., 1966 10-15

Coloring Book, helicopter cover, Whitman, 1969
(figure 2-13) 10-15

Coloring Book, holding basket of pups on cover—
partial re-prints of 1966 version, Whitman,
1973 8-12

Coloring Book, *Landslide at Robbers Range*,
Whitman, 1979 8-12

Coloring Book, *Coloring Book Adventure*, photo
on front & back cover, Whitman, 1960s 10-15

Coloring Book, Fun Book, partial re-prints
of 1960 Whitman coloring book, Merrigold
Press, 1972 8-12

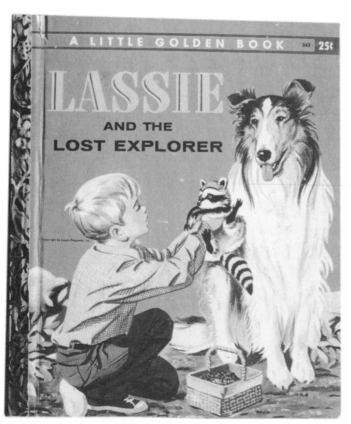

Figure 2-11b

Comic Book, *Adventures of Lassie*, Red Heart
Dog food give-away comic, 1949 . . . . $50-120

Comic Books, Dell Publishing, *M-G-M's Lassie,* painted
covers

1 (photo cover) *(figure 2-14)* 50-100

2 (painted covers begin) *(figure 2-15)* 20-60

3-10 12-35

11-19 10-25

20-36 (last painted covers) *(figure 2-16)* 10-20

37-59 (photo covers) *(figure 2-17, 18, 19)* 5-15

Figure 2-15

Comic Books, Gold Key, *Lassie* (photo covers)

60-69 *(figure 2-20, 21)* 5-15

Comic Books, March of Comics: *Lassie* issues
published 1959-1976

#210, 217, 230 25-32

#308, 324, 334, 370, 381, 394 15-20

#411 (reprint of #324), 432 8-10

Comic Book, Kite fun book, 1973 give-away
comic 15-25

Erasable-Pix Coloring Kit, Timmy and Lassie,
15 x 18-in. box, Standard Toykraft, 1958 60-95

Figure, Breyer Lassie, brown and white plastic
with red tongue, 1950s, unmarked, 6 in. tall
(figure 2-22) 85-100

Figure 2-3

Figure 2-37

Figure 2-16

Figure, Gabriel, fully-articulated Lassie, 1976, from "Lassie and her Friends" playset (*figure 2-23*) $50-85

Figure, Rempel, 8-in. soft rubber squeak toy in 9 x 13-in. box/display stand, 1955 100-150

Figure, unmarked, hollow gold mottled vinyl with "Lassie" on collar, 6 in. 8-12

Footstool, child-sized, Knickerbocker, 1950s 75-100

Halloween Costume (costume, mask, and hood in box), Collegeville, 1956 65-80

Ken-L Ration Gravy Train Dog Food Bag, Lassie on front, 1994 film promo 5-8

Kenner Color Slides—for Give-A-Show Projectors:

Lassie in "Timmy's Bad Break," 1964 3-5

"Lassie the Game Warden," 1966 3-5

Lassie Forest Ranger Kit, mail order: Photos, handbook, wallet, ID cards, badge, etc., 1960s . . 65-95

Lobby Card, *Challenge to Lassie,* MGM, 1950 (scene dependent) 10-15

Lobby Card, *Courage of Lassie*, 1946 (scene dependent) (*figure 2-24*) 20-40

Lobby Card, *Hills of Home*, MGM, 1948 (scene dependent) (*figure 2-25*) 12-20

Lobby Card, *Lassie Come Home*, MGM, 1943 (scene dependent) (*figure 2-26*) 20-40

Lobby Card, *Lassie's Great Adventure,* 20th Century
Fox, 1963 (scene dependent) *(figure 2-27)* $10-12

Lobby Card, *The Painted Hills*, MGM, 1951
(scene dependent) 10-15

Lobby Card, *The Sun Comes Up*, MGM, 1949
(scene dependent) 12-20

Lunch Box, The Magic of Lassie, 1978, King-
Seeley Thermos, steel with blue border
(figure 2-28) 50-65

Figure 2-30

Lunch Kit Thermos, The Magic of Lassie, 1978,
King-Seeley Thermos, blue plastic
(figure 2-28) 10-15

Magazine, *Family Circle*, October 15, 1943,
Lassie cover with Roddy McDowell
(figure 2-29) 15-20

Movie Poster, *Lassie Come Home*, one sheet, MGM
1943 200-300

Movie Poster, *Lassie Come Home*, half sheet/insert,
MGM, 1943 100-200

Movie Poster, *Son of Lassie*, one sheet, MGM
1945 100-150

Movie Poster, *Courage of Lassie*, with Liz Taylor,
one sheet, MGM, 1946 200-300

Movie Poster, *Courage of Lassie*, half sheet/insert,
MGM, 1946 100-200

Figure 2-17

33

Figure 2-14

Movie Poster, *Hills of Home*, one sheet, MGM,
1948 . . . . $70-100

Movie Poster, *The Sun Comes Up*, one sheet,
MGM, 1949 75-125

Movie Poster, *The Sun Comes Up*, half sheet/insert,
MGM, 1949 45-75

Movie Poster, *Challenge to Lassie*, one sheet, MGM,
1950 65-90

Movie Poster, *Challenge to Lassie*, half sheet/insert,
MGM 1950 40-60

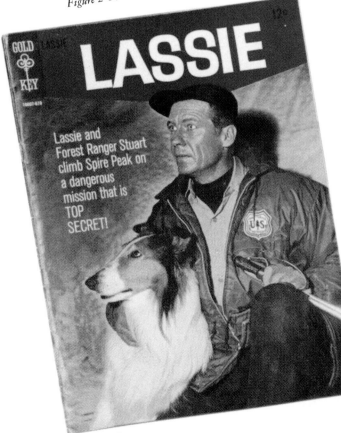

Figure 2-20

Figure 2-21

Movie Poster, *The Painted Hills*, one sheet, MGM,
   1951 . . . .$60-85

Movie Poster, *The Painted Hills*, half sheet/insert,
   MGM, 1951 30-50

Movie Poster, *Lassie's Great Adventure*, one sheet,
   20th Century Fox, 1963 45-75

Movie Poster, *The Magic of Lassie*, one sheet, 1978 . . 35-50

Movie Poster, *Lassie*, one sheet, 1994 15-25

Pet Cologne, Palladium/Carter-Wallace, 8-oz.
   squirt bottle 12-18

Photos, promotional shots issued by CBS with
   program information attached 10-15

Photo, color, 8 x 10 in. on card stock, Recipe
   Brand Dinners give-away, paw print on back 12-20

Figure 2-18

Figure 2-19

Figure 2-22

Figure 2-28

Figure 2-29

Photos, promotional shots with MGM
information and movie title $15-20

Pin-Back Button, photo, "Have You Voted for
Lassie?" 1950s 10-15

Pin-Back Button, "Celebrating the First 50
Years," from the Dog Museum, St. Louis
(figure 2-30) 8-12

Plate, bowl, and plastic glass, Melmac
dinnerware set, Boonton Molding Co. 25-30

Playset, Heartland Farm, 21 pieces including
Jeff, Gramps, Lassie, Marx, 1955 200-400

Playset, Re-issue, Heartland Farm, starring
Lassie, Marx, 1993 60-85

Plush Toy, California Stuffed Toys, Lassie
Television, 21 in., sitting, 1982 35-50

Figure 2-23

Plush Toy, Dakin, Palladium, fur face, 9 1/2 in.
long, 1993 . . . . $10-15

Plush Toy, Dakin, Gravy Train promotion,
red collar with plastic Gravy Train tag, 15 in.,
1993 (figure 2-31) 18-25

Plush Toy, Golden Books Family Entertainment,
Animal Planet promotional toy, 11 in., 3 tags,
1997 20-35

Plush Toy, Gund, 1989 Palladium, fur face,
plastic nose, 2 ft. long, limited edition
(figure 2-32) 40-50

Plush Toy, Knickerbocker, 1965 Wrather Corp.,
flocked plastic face, 2 ft. long (figure 2-33) 50-65

Plush Toy, Knickerbocker, 1965 Wrather Corp.,
plastic face, felt ears, short fur, 1 ft. long
(figure 2-34) 25-35

Plush Toy, Knickerbocker, 1965 Wrather Corp.,
plastic face, yellow photo ribbon, 1.5 ft.
long 35-45

Figure 2-26

Figure 2-24

Figure 2-27

Figure 2-25

Figure 2-35

Plush Toy, unmarked, 1950s-1960s, plastic face,
curved wire in tail, 18 in. long $25-35

Plush Toy, unmarked, 1950s-1960s, short fur,
plastic face, 1 ft. long 20-30

Pogs, set of 6 from 1994 *Lassie* movie 2-3

Poster, "Help Lassie Keep America Beautiful,"
cardboard, 1960s *(figure 2-35)* 25-30

Puzzle, Jr. jigsaw, Lassie with autumn trees,
Whitman, 63 pieces 10-12

Puzzle, Jr. jigsaw, Lassie with sheep, Whitman,
63 pieces *(figure 2-36)* 10-12

Puzzle, jigsaw, Lassie with cougar, Whitman,
1966, 100 pieces 10-12

Puzzle, jigsaw, Lassie with puppies, Whitman,
1971, 100 pieces 8-12

Puzzle, round jigsaw, Lassie with firetruck,
Whitman, 1972, 125 pieces 10-15

Puzzle, frame tray, Lassie with puppies in basket,
Whitman, 1973 8-10

Puzzle, frame tray, Lassie with kids and frisbee,
Whitman, 1980 *(figure 2-37)* 8-10

Figure 2-33

Record, "Lassie Theme Song," Golden Records,
   Sandpipers, Mitch Miller & Orchestra, yellow
   78 rpm $20-25

Record, original radio broadcasts of *The Lassie
   Show*, 33 rpm 35-45

Saturday Evening Post, Dec. 17, 1938, short story,
   "Lassie Come-Home," by Eric Knight 85-100

Saturday Evening Post, Oct. 3, 1964, Lassie photo
   cover (*figure 2-38*) 15-20

Sculpture, "Virgin Mary Lassie," by Dede
   LaRue, 38 in. high, 1991 (*figure 2-39*) 800-1,200

Tennis Shoes, Timmy and Lassie high-tops,
   1950s 75-150

T-Shirt, 50th Anniversary, the Dog Museum
   exclusive, 1993 (*figure 2-40*) 35-45

TV Guide, July 2, 1955, Lassie and Rin Tin
   Tin on cover 30-40

TV Guide, March 1-7, 1958, Hirschfeld portrait
   cover (*figure 2-41*) 15-25

TV Guide, July 4-10, 1959, Timmy and Lassie
   cover (*figure 2-42*) 15-25

Figure 2-36

Figure 2-32

Figure 2-38

Figure 2-42

Figure 2-34

TV Guide, April 30-May 6, 1960, Timmy,
Lassie and mom cover $15-25

TV Guide, August 24-30, 1963, Lassie jumps
fence on cover 15-25

TV Guide, August 14-20, 1965, Lassie and
Ranger Corey on cover 12-20

TV Guide, November 25-Dec. 1, 1972, cover
mentions Lassie cartoons inside 5-10

Video, *Lassie's Rescue Rangers*, Filmation,
1980s 20-35

Figure 2-39

View-Master Packet, 3 reels, "Lassie and Timmy,"
fishing photo cover (B474), Sawyers, 1959 . . . $15-20

View-Master Packet, 3 reels, "Lassie and Timmy,"
mule cover (B474), Sawyers, 1959 15-20

View-Master Packet, 3 reels, "Lassie Look
Homeward" (B480), 1965, GAF Corp. 15-20

View-Master Packet, 3 reels, "Lassie Rides the
Log Flume" (B489), 1968, GAF Corp. 10-15

Wallet, Campbell's Soup mail order give-away,
1959 (figure 2-43) 25-35

Figure 2-41

LASSIE'S 50th ANNIVERSARY
THE DOG MUSEUM

Figure 2-40

Figure 2-31

Figure 2-43

Silver

"Hi-yo, Silver!" is a cry we all remember. When The Lone Ranger was in a jam, Silver could always get him out of it. Following the success of the *Lone Ranger* radio show, which debuted in the early 1930s, CBS aired the *Lone Ranger* television series from 1949-1961, starring Clayton Moore and Jay Silverheels.

In 1954, George Trendle sold all *Lone Ranger* rights, scripts and shows to Jack Wrather, who produced *Lassie*. The $3 million purchase price made it the biggest TV deal of its kind to date at that time.

During the final years of the TV series, two feature films were made: *The Lone Ranger* (1956, Warner Brothers) and *The Lone Ranger and the City of Gold* (1958, United Artists). Decades later, in 1981, another film, *The Legend of the Lone Ranger* was released. Silver was also prominently featured in both of *The Lone Ranger* cartoon series, one which aired in the late 1960s and one which debuted in 1980.

According to the original radio script, the Lone Ranger was riding over the plains one day, when he came upon a beautiful wild white stallion, engaged in a fierce battle to the death with a raging buffalo. He had heard legends of a fiery white stallion who ruled a herd of wild horses in the area. Seeing that the horse was losing the battle, the Lone Ranger fired two silver bullets into the huge black buffalo, killing it immediately. After the Lone Ranger and Tonto nursed the badly wounded horse back to health, they decided to set it free. But, the horse had other ideas. Now tame and gentle, he chose to stay with his protector. "Him shine like Silver," noted Tonto. And "Silver" became his name.

One of the most popular horses of all time, Silver had his own long-running comic book line. Other Silver collectibles include action figures, plush toys, Hartland figures, kid's books, puzzles, and much more.

Silver Collectibles Price Guide

Bandanna, Hi-Yo Silver, printed fabric, 22.5 x
21.5 in., Cheerios premium, 1949-1950 . . . . . $50-75

Bank, Lone Ranger Strong Box, metal, 3.5 in.,
1938 80-130

Book, *The Red Renegades*, Better Little Book,
Whitman, 1939 35-50

Book, *The Great Western Span*, Better Little Book,
Whitman, 1942 35-50

Book, *The Secret Weapon*, Better Little Book,
Whitman, 1943 35-50

Book, *The Lone Ranger and His Horse Silver*,
Big Little Book, Whitman, 1935 35-50

Book, *The Vanishing Herd*, Big Little Book,
Whitman, 1936 35-50

Book, *Heigh-Yo Silver!* 8.5 x 11.5 in., Dell
Publishing, 10¢ cover price, 1938 75-125

Book, *The Lone Ranger*, die-cut paper, Random
House, 1981 8-15

Book, *The Lone Ranger*, Little Golden Book 263,
1956 15-20

Figure 3-7

Figure 3-1

Book, *The Lone Ranger and the Talking Pony*, Little Golden Book 310, 1958 .... $15-20

Book, *The Lone Ranger and the Ghost Horse*, Whitman Tell-A-Tale Book, 1955 (*figure 3-1*) 6-10

Book, *The Lone Ranger and the War Horse*, Whitman Cozy Corner Book, 1950s 8-12

Book, *The Lone Ranger*, Pop-Up Book, Random House, 1981 (*figure 3-2*) 12-20

Book, *The Lone Ranger Rocking Book*, 7.5 x 9.5 in., bottom is curved 35-50

Brush, military brush set, boxed, no handle, 1939 50-85

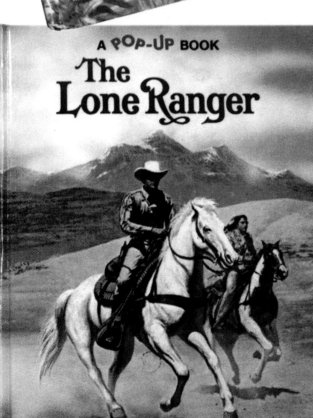

Figure 3-2

Figure 3-3

Chalkware Carnival Figure, Lone Ranger on Silver,
11 in., 1940s $75-125

Coloring Book, *Hi-Yo Silver*, Silver rearing on cover,
6.5 x 7.5 in., Whitman, 1955 20-30

Comic Book, *Hi-Yo Silver*, Dell
#1 (Dell Four Color #369), 1951 *(figure 3-3)* . . . 30-90

#2 (Dell Four Color #392), 1952 *(figure 3-4)* . . . 15-45

#3-#10 *(figure 3-5)* 12-35

#11-#36 *(figure 3-6—3-14)* 10-25

Comic Book, *The Lone Ranger* (Dell Publishing)
#102, December 1956 *(figure 3-15)* 15-45

#127, photo cover, April/May 1959
(figure 3-16) 30-75

Figure 3-8

Figure 3-4

Figure 3-9

Figure 3-10

Figure 3-11

Figure 3-12

Comic Book, *Lone Ranger Movie Story*, Dell
 Giant, 1956 . . . . $125-200

Comic Book, *The Lone Ranger* (Gold Key) #5,
 January 1967 *(figure 3-17)* 3-9

Comic Book, *Lone Ranger Comics*, #1, Lone
 Ranger Ice Cream Cones Premium,
 1938 600-800

Comic Book, *The Lone Ranger and the Story
 of Silver*, 2.5 x 7-in. Cheerios give-away
 (figure 3-18) 45-100

Figure, Scout, legs move, removable saddle and
 reins, 5 in., Gabriel, 1980 *(figure 3-19)* 15-25

Figure, Scout, legs move, Empire Toys, Carolina
 Enterprises, 4 in., 1970s *(figure 3-20)* 10-15

Figure, Scout with Tonto, 12 in., articulated
 plastic with accessories, Gabriel, 1977 40-75

Figure, Scout with Tonto, 9.5 in., standing,
 Hartland Plastics, boxed, 1954 100-250

Figure, Scout with Tonto, 9.5 in., semi-rearing
 pose, Hartland Plastics, boxed, 1954 200-350

Figure, Silver & Lone Ranger, 12 in., articulated
 plastic with accessories, Gabriel, 1977
 (figure 3-21) 40-75

Figure, Silver, "Legend of the Lone Ranger" card,
Gabriel, 1979 . . . . $30-45

Figure, Silver with Lone Ranger, Hartland
Plastics, 5.5 in., 1960 40-100

Figure, standing Silver with Lone Ranger,
Hartland Plastics, 9.5 in., boxed, 1954 200-300

Figure, half-rearing Silver with Lone Ranger,
Hartland Plastics, 9.5 in., boxed, 1950s 150-250

Figure, rearing Silver with Lone Ranger,
Hartland Plastics, 9.5 in., boxed, 1954
(figure 3-22) 200-300

Figure, Smoke, black horse with white socks,
5 in., Gabriel, 1979 30-45

First Aid Kit, tin litho case, 4 x 6 in., White
Cross Labs, 1938 50-75

Game, "Lone Ranger, Hi-Yoooo Silver!"
board game, Parker Bros., 1938 60-85

Game, "Hi-Yo Silver, Lone Ranger Card Game,"
3.5 x 5-in. box, Parker Bros., 1938 50-75

Game, "Lone Ranger and the Silver Bullets,"
13.5 x 16 in., 1956 60-80

Glass, Hi-Yo Silver, Silver rears with Lone Ranger
on back, 5 in.-tumbler, 1938 80-120

Figure 3-15

Figure 3-16

Figure 3-17

Figure 3-6

Figure 3-5

Guitar, Hi-Yo Silver/Lone Ranger, pressed wood,
Superior Musical Instruments, 1940s $150-200

Lunch Box, The Lone Ranger, Hi-Yo Silver,
ADCO Liberty, 1954, red sides version 200-300

Lunch Box, The Lone Ranger, Hi-Yo Silver,
ADCO Liberty, 1954, blue sides version 250-400

Lunch Box, The Lone Ranger, Hi-Yo Silver, 1990s
reproduction by G Whiz *(figure 3-23, 24)* 20-30

Lunch Box, Legend of the Lone Ranger, with
thermos, Aladdin, 1980 30-55

Magazine, *Jack and Jill*, "Hi-Yo, Silver,
Away-y-y!" October 1960 3-5

Model Kit, Lone Ranger, Silver rears up, 1/10
scale, Aurora, 1967 20-150

Model Kit, Lone Ranger, comic scenes series,
re-release of above, Aurora, 1974 *(figure 3-25)* . . 20-25

Movie Poster, *Hi-Yo Silver*, Republic, 1940 100-150

Movie Poster, *The Lone Ranger* (1938 serial,
Republic, 15 chapters) 2,000-3,000

Movie Poster, *The Lone Ranger*, Warner Bros.,
1956 250-350

Movie Poster, *The Lone Ranger and the Lost
City of Gold*, Warner Bros., 1958 . . . . $100-200

Paddle-Ball, Hi-Yo Silver Lone Ranger Bat-O-Ball,
from Tom's Toasted Peanuts, 1939 100-150

Paint Book, Hi-Yo Silver, 11 x 14 in.,
Whitman, 1938 65-95

Paint Box, tin litho with paints inside, Milton
Bradley, 1950s 35-60

Photograph, Silver head shot with Lone Ranger,
8 x 10 in., B&W, Merita bread, 1940s 75-100

Photograph, Silver and Lone Ranger with Tonto
and Scout, color, 8 x 10 in., 1950s 15-25

Picture Printing Kit, rubber stamps and booklet,
Stamperkraft, 1939 80-120

Pin-Back Button, "Hi-Yo Silver—The Lone Ranger,"
photo, 1930s 50-75

Pin-Back Button, "Member-Lone Ranger Safety
Club," 1930s 25-50

Playset, Lone Ranger Rodeo, 13 x 15-in. box,
Marx, 1950 150-250

Figure 3-13

Figure 3-14

Figure 3-18

Pocketknife, Silver, with illustration, 3.5 in.,
Paladium, 1993 *(figure 3-26)* $12-20

Program Book, "Millions of eyes are on . . . The
Lone Ranger," from first feature film, 1956 . . 175-225

Push Puppet, plastic Silver figure with Lone
Ranger on back, 2-in. round base, 1968 40-65

Figure 3-19

Puzzle, frame tray, Silver and Lone Ranger run
across desert, 15 x 11 in., Whitman 25-35

Puzzle, frame tray, Silver and Scout with Lone
Ranger and Tonto, Whitman, 1954 25-35

Puzzle, photo of Silver in foreground with Lone
Ranger and Tonto, 1978 12-20

Puzzles, jigsaw, boxed set of 3, Puzzle Craft,
1945 100-150

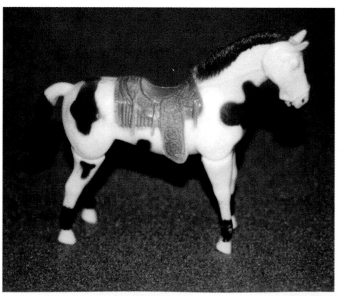

Figure 3-20

Radio, bakelite with Silver and Lone Ranger
on dial face, Pilot, late 1930s 800-1,200

Radio, plastic with relief figures of Silver and
Lone Ranger, 6 in., Majestic, 1950s 750-1,000

Record, "Lone Ranger—He Finds Silver," 78 or
45 rpm, Decca, 1951-52 20-30

Record Set, full series of 8, 78 or 45 rpm,
Decca, 1951-52 . . . . $150-200

Rocking Horse, Hi-Yo Silver! 21 in. tall,
painted wood, 1940s 250-350

School Bag, cloth and vinyl, Hi-Yo Silver,
shoulder strap, 1950s 100-150

Scrapbook, cover shows Lone Ranger with lasso
on Silver, 11 x 15.5 in., 1940s 50-65

Scrapbook, cover shows Lone Ranger on Silver,
galloping, 10 x 13.5 in., Whitman, 1950s 25-40

Spoon, Silver and Lone Ranger on handle, silver-
plate, 1938 40-65

Target Game, Tin stand-up of Silver and Lone
Ranger, 9.5 x 9.5-in. box, Marx, 1938 225-300

Target Game, tin litho, 16 x 27 in., Marx,
1938 250-325

Target Game, color cardboard square target,
Marx, 1946 90-160

Tattoo Transfers, with bubble gum, by Swell,
1970s 12-20

Trading Card, Ed-U-Cards, 1950s, individual card . . 2-4

Figure 3-21

Tie, Hi-Yo Silver graphic, rayon, The Lone Ranger
Inc., 1939 . . . .$ 50-75

Tin Toy, Hi-Yo Silver, the Lone Ranger, wind-up,
lasso spins, 7 in., boxed, Marx, 1938 350-700

Tin Toy, Range Rider, wind-up, rocker base,
9.5 in., Marx, 1950s revamp of above 200-350

Tin Toy, Scout and Tonto, 1950s, 6 in. 75-100

Toothbrush Holder, Silver rearing with Lone
Ranger on back, composition, 4 in., 1938 75-125

View-Master Packet, "The Lone Ranger," 3-reel
set, GAF, 1956 25-35

Figure 3-22

Figure 3-23

View-Master Packet, "Legend of the Lone Ranger,"
3-reel set, 1981 . . . . $10-15

Wallet, Lone Ranger sign, Hi-Yo Silver, brown
vinyl, color artwork, 1953 65-95

Watch, lapel watch, boxed with leather holster
strap fob, New Haven, 1940 300-450

Watch, pocket watch, "Hi-Yo Silver" word
bubble, 2 in. diameter, New Haven, 1939 . . . 300-450

Watch, wrist watch, Lone Ranger rides Silver on
face, silver trim, brown band, 1950s 100-200

Watch, wrist watch, tin and fake leather toy
watch, square face, 1950s 50-75

Figure 3-25

Figure 3-24

Figure 3-26

Smokey Bear

Smokey Bear began his legacy, not as a live animal star, but as a graphic on an advertising poster. The poster, commissioned in 1944 by the Cooperative Forest Fire Prevention Campaign, featured Albert Staehle's artwork depicting a bear pouring water over a campfire. He was named after "Smokey Joe" Martin, an assistant chief with the New York City Fire Department.

The poster was a hit, and Staehle followed it up with two more during the next two years. The most memorable, issued in 1947, introduced the plea, "Remember! Only You Can Prevent Forest Fires." Rudy Wendelin was the second official Smokey artist, and he created Smokey posters and ads for thirty years. Wendelin's Smokey seemed cuddlier than his predecessor, with a more humanized look, and a shorter nose.

The living Smokey Bear was discovered in spring, 1950, a frightened black bear cub clinging to a smoking, charred tree in the aftermath of a forest fire. The fire, which blazed through New Mexico's Lincoln National Forest, separated the four-pound cub from his mother, leaving him badly burned and dazed. The firefighters who rescued the cub took him to Santa Fe veterinarian Dr. E. J. Smith, who treated the cub's wounds. He was named Smokey, after the popular poster bear, because he embodied the very lesson that the Forest Service was trying to teach.

Smokey was not, however, a very cooperative patient. Under the care of Ray Bell (of the New Mexico Department of Fish and Game), Smokey refused to eat, until Ray's wife concocted a mixture of instant baby food and honey. And, while Smokey recuperated, he developed a love/hate relationship with Ray Bell, who had the unpleasant task of changing the cub's bandages. The process was an arduous and painful one, and Smokey would often retaliate by biting Ray. As Smokey grew, this became a more serious dilemma.

Finally, in June, Ray Bell and his group decided to donate Smokey to the National Zoological Park in Washington D.C. America loved Smokey, and he soon became one of the zoo's star attractions, promoting forest fire prevention and winning the hearts of kids and adults alike.

The bear's popularity soon moved Smokey's "owners" to promote a new law, called The Smokey Bear Act, assuring that any items produced or sold using Smokey's name or image be approved by the Secretary of Agriculture. The law, passed in May 1952, also stated that any fees collected using Smokey's image be placed in a special account to promote forest fire prevention.

Following the new law, the first licensed Smokey Bear plush toy was produced in 1953 by the Ideal Toy Company. The brown plush bear had a vinyl face, and he sported blue jeans, and a silver metal badge and belt buckle. He carried a blue plastic shovel.

Ideal released several more plush Smokeys, but the company's most ingenious move was to include application cards allowing kids to become a "Junior Forest Ranger." The Forest Service was besieged with such an onslaught of responses that Smokey Bear Headquarters was given its own zip code (20252) in Washington, D.C.

Knickerbocker also produced a line of plush Smokey Bears in the 1950s and 1960s. Often, when tags are pulled off the bears, collectors have a tough time telling Knickerbocker bears from Ideal bears. Here's the main difference: Knickerbocker's Smokey Badge shows Smokey's face and says "Smokey Ranger." Ideal's Smokey Badges have type with no portrait.

In the 1960s, Knickerbocker issued a series of Smokey Bear toys with a different kind of face—cuter, with a sort of Disney-ish influence, designed by an artist named Berryman. These toys, distinctive in their design, are now simply referred to as "Berryman Face" Smokeys.

In September 1969, ABC launched *The Smokey Bear Show*, an animated ecology cartoon show produced by Rankin-Bass, which aired until September 1971.

Smokey Bear died in 1976, outliving the average bear by more than a decade. He was buried near his birthplace, at Smokey Bear Historical State Park in New Mexico.

The Forest Service was forced to embark on a new campaign, pointing out that Smokey and his message were still "alive." Afterwards, the decision was made to nix the live bear routine, and stick with graphics and animated messages.

Smokey Bear Collectibles Price Guide

Figure 4-1

Animation Cel, from TV Forestry ad, Atkinson Film Arts, 11.5 x 14 in., 1980s *(figure 4-1)* . . $100-200

Animation Cel, from *The Smokey Bear Show*, Rankin-Bass, 1969-71 150-250

Ash Tray, round, yellow with raised face, "Smokey Says Prevent Forest Fires," 7 in. *(figure 4-2)* 50-75

Figure 4-2

Ash Tray, kidney-shaped with figural Smokey holding shovel, Norcrest, late 1960s 65-90

Ash Tray, kidney-shaped with figural Smokey breaking match, Norcrest, late 1960s *(figure 4-3)* 65-90

Ash Tray, kidney-shaped with figural Smokey holding pail, Norcrest, late 1960s 65-90

Ash Tray, "Be Careful With Smokes," green ceramic base, 4 x 4 in., Norcrest, late 1970s . . . 65-90

Figure 4-3

Ash Tray, round, portrait with shovel, 4.25 in., Cameron of California, only 20 made 60-80

Ash Tray, Intl. Falls, MN, picture of Smokey statue built in 1954, 7.25 in. 20-35

Backpack, green and brown with Smokey Bear face, 1990s 20-35

Badge, Junior Forest Ranger, 1950s 12-20

Bank, ceramic, white with gold glitter tone,
7.5 in., 1950s $90-120

Bank, ceramic, same as above, full color with
gold glitter tone, 7.5 in., 1950s 90-120

Bank, figural, holds sign, "Prevent Forest Fires,"
14 in., Play Pal Plastics, Inc., 1972 *(figure 4-4)* . . 45-65

Bank, Smokey on Cut Tree with Shovel, 10.5 in.,
plastic with jeans, Dakin, 1971 *(figure 4-5)* 50-75

Bank, "Save with Smokey," waving figural, plastic
give-away piece, 8.5 in. *(figure 4-6)* 45-65

Figure 4-4

Figure 4-6

Figure 4-5

Figure 4-7

Bank, composition, bright paint, 10 in.,
Norcrest, 1970s $80-120

Bank, Smokey Ranger Station, 4 x 5 in.-log
cabin, Child Lore Co., late 1970s (*figure 4-7*) . . . 50-75

Bank, ceramic figural, 10 in., Treasure Craft/
Cookie Jarrin, 1996 (*figure 4-8 left*) 35-50

Bank, ceramic head, 6 in., Treasure Craft/Cookie
Jarrin, 1996 (*figure 4-8 right*) 35-45

Figure 4-8

Figure 4-9

Figure 4-10

Bank, Smokey figural sitting with shovel, china,
6.5 in., Norcrest, 1970s *(figure 4-9 right)* $40-55

Bank, Smokey figural sitting with pail, china,
6.5 in., Norcrest, 1970s *(figure 4-9 left)* 40-55

Bank, figural plastic, standing with shovel,
10 in., IML, 1970s *(figure 4-10)* 35-50

Bank, die-cast Ertl truck, 1990s, ltd. edition 30-40

Bank, die-cast Ertl truck, 1990s, ltd. edition 30-40

Bank, die-cast Ertl truck, 1990s, ltd. edition 30-40

Figure 4-11

Figure 4-13

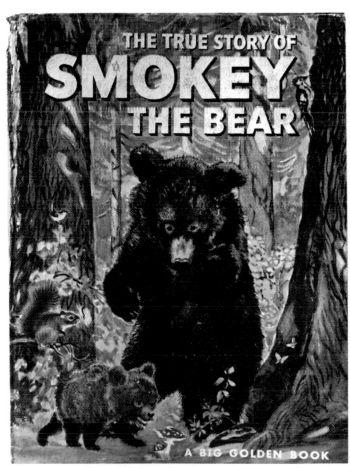

Figure 4-14

59

Figure 4-16

Bathroom accessories, ceramic, 1990s *(figure 4-11)*
    Kleenex Dispenser (figural head) $25-40

    Toothbrush Holder (figural head) 12-20

    Cup 8-12

    Soft Soap Dispenser (figural) 12-20

    Round Soap Dish, "Only You Can Prevent . . ." . . 8-12

    Waste Basket 25-40

Beach Ball, 13 in., inflatable, Tennie G, 1979
    (figure 4-12) 20-30

Blanket, Dewey Trading Co. exclusive, Santa Fe,
    by Pendleton, 1994 *(figure 4-13)* 165-200

Figure 4-17

Figure 4-15

Book, *Smokey the Bear*, Little Golden Book 224,
1955 . . . .$10-15

Book, *Smokey Bear and the Campers*, Little Golden
Book 423, 1961 6-10

Book, *Smokey Bear Finds a Helper*, Little Golden
Book 345, 1972 5-8

Book, *Smokey and His Animal Friends,* Little
Golden Book 387, 1960 8-12

Book, *The True Story of Smokey the Bear*, Big
Golden Book, 1955 *(figure 4-14)* 10-15

Bubble Bath Container, 11.5 in., Lander Co. Inc.,
1960s-1970s 35-50

Figure 4-18

Figure 4-20

Figure 4-19

Figure 4-22

Bubble Bath Container, "Soaky," 9 in., Colgate-
Palmolive Co., 1960s $30-45

Button, tab button, "I'm Helping Smokey,"
Green Duck Co., Chicago, 1940s 20-30

Figure 4-23

Carving, licensed hand-carved Smokey face in
real wood, ltd. edition award, rare
(figure 4-15) 150-200

Charcoal Lighter Fluid Can, Smokey Bear, with
picture, Husky Industries, Atlanta 25-40

Christmas Ornament, ceramic, 40th Anniversary,
2,000 made, Cameron of California, 1984 65-80

Coca Cola Collectors Exclusive Pieces—for 50th
Anniversary (figure 4-16)
    Plush toy, 12 in., 400 made 175-225

Figure 4-24

Figure 4-21

Plush Toy, 15 in., 2,000 made $150-200

Coke Bottle with Smokey Portrait *(figure 4-16)* . . 25-35

Decorative Tin Litho Tray *(figure 4-16)* 75-100

Playing Cards, sealed in package *(figure 4-16)* . . . 30-45

Comic Book, *Forest Fire*, 1950, American
Forestry Assn., 1st appearance of Smokey 50-120

Comic Book, March of Comics series, 5 x 7 in., store give-
away
#234 10-20

#362, 372 (based on TV show) 5-10

#383 (based on TV show) 4-8

#407 (based on TV show) 3-5

Figure 4-25

Figure 4-26

Figure 4-28

Comic Book, *Smokey Bear*, based on TV show, Gold Key, 1970-73

  #1 .... $4-8

  #2-13 2-5

Comic Book, *Smokey the Bear* (from Dell Four-Color series), Dell Publishing

  #653 (#1), October 1955 30-100

  #708, 754, 818, 932 15-50

  #1016, 1119, 1214 10-40

  #229 15-50

Comic Book, *The True Story of Smokey Bear*, Forest Service give-away, 1959, 1st print 8-15

Comic Book, *The True Story of Smokey Bear*, Forest Service give-away, reprint 2-5

Figure 4-29

Figure 4-27

Cookie Jar, 50th Anniversary, only 250 made,
15 in., Treasure Craft/Cookie Jarrin, 1994
(*figure 4-17*) $300-400

Cookie Jar, Smokey head, ltd. edition, Treasure
Craft/Cookie Jarrin, 1995 150-200

Cup, figural Smokey handle, ceramic, Norcrest,
1970s 45-65

Cup, ceramic, Norcrest, 1970s 45-65

Drinking Glass Set, cold drink makes green trees
appear, set of 4 12-oz. glasses, 1990s 30-40

Figure, plastic, Smokey on Tree Stump, Dakin,
1971 50-75

Figure 4-31

Figure 4-32

Figure 4-30

Figure 4-33

Figure, plastic, Smokey, in Cartoon Theater box,
Dakin, 1976 . . . . $40-65

Figurine, ceramic, 3.5 in., three designs (shovel,
pail, broken match), Norcrest, each 65-90

Figurine, ceramic, set of 3 (match, shovel, pail),
2 in., Norcrest, 1970s, set *(figure 4-18)* 80-100

Figurine, bronze tone ceramic, 9.5 in., The Great
Razooly, 1993 40-50

Figurine, hand-painted china, Smokey and Deer,
5.25 in., Lefton, 1996 18-25

Figure 4-34

Figure 4-35

Figurine, hand-painted china, Smokey's Mailbox,
5.5 in., Lefton, 1996 . . . . $18-25

Figurine, hand-painted china, Smokey Relaxing,
4.25 in., Lefton, 1996 8-25

Figurine, hand-painted china, Backpacking
Smokey, 5 in., Lefton, 1996 20-28

Figurine, hand-painted china, Cubs with
Watering Can, 4.25 in., Lefton, 1996 18-25

Figurine, hand-painted china, Smokey, Cubs by
Stream, 5.5 in., Lefton, 1996 22-30

Figurine, hand-painted china, Smokey Teaching,
5.25 in., Lefton, 1996 26-35

Figurine, hand-painted china, Fire Prevention
signs, 5.5 in., Lefton, 1996 20-28

Game, "Smokey: Forest Fire Prevention Bear,"
Ideal, 1961 75-125

Game, "Smokey the Bear Game," Milton Bradley,
1968 (figure 4-19) 50-80

Gripper, 2.25 in., plush, ITI Hawaii Inc., 1979 . . 10-15

Inflatable Toy, 23 in., Tennie G., Taiwan, 1979 . . . 25-40

Lawn Ornament, 14 in., plastic molded figure,
Art Line, 1979 30-45

Figure 4-40

Figure 4-42

Figure 4-41

Lawn Ornament, Smokey holds sign, "Prevent
Forest Fires," 1977 . . . . $30-45

Lunch Box, 50th Anniversary, plastic, Little
John Collectibles/Thermos, 1994 (*figure 4-20*) . . 35-50

Lunch Box, plastic, "Put the Crunch on Wildfires,"
Minnesota Timber wolves, radio promo 35-50

Lunch Box, plastic, Rockford Royals, 50th
Anniversary promo, Illinois 35-45

Lunch Box, steel, with thermos, Okay, 1975 . . . 300-500

Mug, ceramic, 4.75 in., only 12 made,
Cameron of California, 1984 75-100

Music Box, hand-painted china, Smokey in Jeep/
Country Road, 6 in., Lefton, 1996 25-40

Music Box, hand-painted china, Smokey in Bed/
Brahms' Lullaby, 5 in., Lefton, 1996 25-40

Nesting Toy (Matryoshka), Smokey and Friends,
6.25 in., from Eastern Russia (*figure 4-21*) 30-50

Nodder, 6 in., composition, round, white base,
bright body, Norcrest, 1960s 120-150

Pajama Bag, fake fur, Smokey's face, with hat 30-45

Pin-Back Button, hot pink, "Only You Can
Prevent Forest Fires," with face 2-5

Pin-Back Button, "A Pledge to the Careful . . . ,"
   giveaway, 1946 (*figure 4-22*) $20-25

Playset, "Camping the Smokey Bear Way,"
   Tonka, with toys & book, 10 x 17-in. box, 1973
   (*figure 4-23*) 100-200

Plush Toy, first Smokey toy ever produced, 16 in.,
   with metal badge, buckle, Ideal, 1953
   (*figure 4-24*) 250-350

Plush Toy, second made, 21 in., plastic face
   and hat, Ideal, 1954 200-300

Plush Toy, sitting, vinyl face, glassine eyes,
   plastic badge and hat, Ideal, 1956
   (*figure 4-25*) 150-200

Plush Toy, "Official Smokey the Bear," 12 in.,
   boxed, Ideal, 1967 65-95

Plush Toy, with felt eyes, 18 in., Ideal, 1957
   (*figure 4-26*) 90-120

Plush Toy, plastic eyes, 18 in., Ideal, 1957
   (*figure 4-26*) 90-120

Plush Toy, plastic eyes, 14 in., Ideal, 1957
   (*figure 4-26*) 65-85

Plush Toy, 31 in., (shown with no hat or badge),
   plastic belt, Knickerbocker, early 1960s 75-125

Plush Toy, 25 in. (plastic hat, belt and badge),
   denim legs, Knickerbocker, early 1960s
   (*figure 4-27*) 90-130

Figure 4-38

Figure 4-39

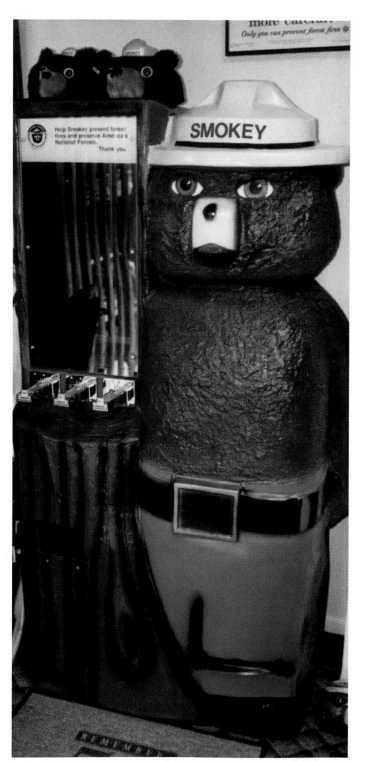

Figure 4-47

Plush Toy, sitting version, 14 in., plastic accessories, Knickerbocker, early 1960s (*figure 4-28*) $70-100

Plush Toy, Berryman face, 30 in., (shown with missing hat) Knickerbocker, late 1960s 125-175

Plush Toy, Berryman face, 35 in., (shown with missing hat) Knickerbocker, late 1960s (*figure 4-29*) 150-200

Plush Toy, Berryman face, 21 in., Knickerbocker, late 1960s 75-100

Plush Toy, all cloth, 7 in., boxed, Knickerbocker, 1972 30-50

Plush Toy, 15 in., wearing "Think" T-shirt, mouth open, Dakin, 1977 60-90

Plush Toy, 10 in., plastic tag in front, red cardboard tag, Dakin, 1980 (*figure 4-30*) 40-55

Plush Toy, 15 in., plastic tag in front, red cardboard tag, Dakin, 1980 50-65

Plush Toy, 12 in., two versions—one with felt feet, Dakin, 1985, each (*figure 4-31*) 25-40

Plush Toy, 7 in., The Three Bears Co., 1985 20-30

Plush Toy, 14.5 in., The Three Bears Co., 1985 . . . 30-40

Plush Toy, 15.5 in., The Three Bears Co., 1985 . . $40-60

Plush Toy, 31 in., all cloth and plush, removable
clothes, The Three Bears Co., 1985
(*figure 4-32*) 150-200

Plush Toy, 50th Anniversary, 9.5 in., felt hat,
leatherette belt, Bon Ton, 1994 (*figure 4-33*) 30-40

Plush Toy, 12 in. bear with plastic shovel, felt
hat, ltd. edition, Intl. Bon Ton, boxed, 1994 . . . 30-40

Figure 4-12

Plush Toy, 50th Anniversary, 21 in., wooden
shovel, felt hat, ltd. ed., JJ Wind, 1994
(*figure 4-34*) 55-75

Plush Toy, "Official Book and Bear Set," 8 in.
bear with book, boxed, Bon Ton, 1996
(*figure 4-35*) 18-25

Poster, first Smokey product ever produced,
20 x 14 in., by Albert Staehle, 1944
(*figure 4-36*) 300-450

Posters, various designs, 1970s-1990s, each
(*figure 4-37*) 20-40

Powder Box, ceramic with removable lid,
Cameron of California, ltd. edition, 1990s 50-65

Puppet, 12 in., plush with felt hat, 1990s 20-30

Puzzle, 20-in. diameter round jigsaw,
125 pieces, Whitman, 1970 (*figure 4-38*) 15-25

Figure 4-43

Figure 4-48

Figure 4-45

Puzzle, 100-piece jigsaw, 14 x 18 in.,
Whitman, 1971 (*figure 4-39*) $12-20

Record, 78 rpm, picture sleeve, Peter Pan
Records, 1960 15-25

Rocking Chair, wood, 50th Anniversary,
Nichols and Stone, Ohio, 1994 only 350-450

Salt & Pepper Shakers, china, 3.5 in. holding
shovel/bucket, Norcrest, Japan, late 1960s
(*figure 4-40*) 45-65

Salt & Pepper Shakers, china, 4 in. holding
shovel/bucket, Norcrest, Japan, late 1960s
(*figure 4-41*) 45-65

Salt & Pepper Shakers, china, 4.5 in. holding
shovel/bucket, Norcrest, Japan, late 1960s
(*figure 4-42*) 45-65

Salt & Pepper Shakers, china, Smokey heads,
Norcrest, Japan, late 1960s 60-75

Salt & Pepper Shakers, salt in face/pepper in hat,
5 in., Treasure Craft/Cookie Jarrin, 1996
(*figure 4-43*) 30-40

Stained Glass, 50th Anniversary, only 50 made,
17.25 in., octagon (*figure 4-44*) 200-300

Talking Smokey, 15 in. (plastic hat, belt, badge),
says 16 things, Knickerbocker, 1960s
(*figure 4-45*) 65-95

Talking Smokey, plush with Berryman face,
16 in., Knickerbocker, late 1960s $65-95

Talking Smokey, 14 in., felt hat, leatherette
belt, JC Penney exclusive, Bon Ton, 1995 50-75

Tent, Fun Tent, child size, plastic, Industrial
Safety Belt Co., 1970s 50-85

Thermos, King Seeley (went with vinyl lunch
box), 1965 (*figure 4-46*) 40-50

Truck, Smokey's Ranger Vehicle—jeep, steel,
Tonka, 1973 (part of playset) 35-50

Truck, Smokey's Ranger Vehicle—station
wagon, steel, Tonka, 1973 (part of playset) 35-50

Truck, Smokey's Ranger Vehicle—hauling
truck, steel, Tonka, 1973 (part of playset) 35-50

Vending Machine, Figural Smokey on left
side, 64 in., 1990 (*figure 4-47*) 2,500-3,500

Watch, Hawthorne, dial face shows Smokey,
"Prevent Forest Fires," late 1960s 65-100

Watch, pocket watch, Bradley, late 1970s
(*figure 4-48*) 150-200

Watch, wrist watch, hands are matches, Bradley,
late 1970s 100-150

Figure 4-46

Figure 4-44

Trigger

Stuffed and mounted in the Roy Rogers museum, Trigger, himself, may be the most coveted of all animal star collectibles (but don't count on him being offered for sale any time soon). Also stuffed beside Trigger are Trigger, Jr.; Dale's horse, Buttermilk; and Bullet, the Wonder Dog.

Trigger's popularity was phenomenal during the 1950s, and the horse starred in films like *My Pal Trigger* and *Trigger, Jr.*, as well as Roy Rogers' other films—nearly 90 in all. Dubbed "The smartest horse in the movies," Trigger usually got second billing, ahead of Dale Evans. On *The Roy Rogers Show* (NBC, 1951-57), Trigger acted alongside Buttermilk and Bullet (a German shepherd), appearing in more than 100 episodes.

Trigger's amazing career began in 1938, when a young Roy Rogers was to star in a new cowboy picture called *Under Western Stars*. Roy got to audition his own horse, and third in the line-up was a beautiful palomino named Golden Cloud, son of a racehorse named Caliente. In a 1976 interview with the author, Roy recalled, "I knew I wanted a palomino to start with. The third horse they showed me was Trigger. I hadn't liked the first two, but when I took ol' Trigger for a test ride, I told 'em he was the one I wanted. I didn't even look at any of the others."

It was the horse of his dreams. Not only did he elect to ride the horse in the new film, he bought Golden Cloud for $2,500. He liked the way the horse handled, and its amazing speed; "quick as a trigger," to be exact. And so, Golden Cloud earned a new name. He was Trigger.

Roy's instincts for horse selection turned out to be uncanny. He and Trigger grew close enough to cause Dale a certain amount of actual envy. Trigger thrived under the attention and training of the young cowboy, and, eventually, learned to count up to 25 by stamping his hoof. Roy insisted that Trigger could also perform simple subtraction and multiplication problems, and he reportedly did so in front of more than a few audiences. Trigger learned to walk on his hind legs for about 150 feet, and could even sign an "X" in a hotel register book. More amazingly, he was also house trained, a trick which the hotels, no doubt, appreciated.

Today, there are no direct descendants of Trigger. Roy believed that fatherhood might make Trigger less gentle to people. "My kids could walk right under his belly and it wouldn't bother him," Roy explained. "He was real gentle, and I wanted to keep him that way."

Trigger Jr., then, was not actually Trigger's colt. Junior, however, did have many kids of his own. A third Trigger also existed, although he was never widely publicized. "Little Trigger" was used as Trigger's stand-in, and frequently traveled to promotional appearances, allowing the "real" Trigger to relax.

Trigger lived to be 33. "He's not really stuffed," Roy explained. "They don't do that anymore. It's the same way they do the large animals at the Smithsonian Institute. They make a fiberglass of the animal and put the hide over it. I'd seen what happened to you when you're put underground, and I just couldn't see ol' Trigger being shoveled under the dirt like that. He meant so much to so many people."

Today, collectors seek Trigger figures, lunch boxes, lamps, books, comics, movie posters, lobby cards, magazine appearances, photos and more. Like Silver and Gene Autry's Champion, Trigger was also featured in his own line of comic books.

Trigger Collectibles Price Guide

Alarm Clock, Roy and Trigger move on face,
 Ingraham Co., boxed, 1951 *(figure 5-1)* $150-250

Bandanna, Roy and Trigger, 17 x 17 in., 1950s . . . 50-75

Bank, pastel-colored china, 7.5 in., late 1940s . .150-250

Bedspread, made with Roy Rogers fabric 125-200

Book, *Bullet and Trigger   Wild Horse Roundup*,
 Whitman, 1953 20-30

Book, *Roy Rogers and the Mountain Lion*, Little
 Golden Book 231, 1955 15-20

Book, *Roy Rogers and the New Cowboy*, Little
 Golden Book 177, 1953 15-20

Book, *Roy Rogers and the Indian Sign*, Little
 Golden Book 259, 1956 15-20

Book, *Roy Rogers—King of the Cowboys*, Big
 Golden Book, 1950s *(figure 5-2)* 20-30

Book, *Roy Rogers Cowboy Annual*, British,
 hardcover, 7 x 10 in., 1952 55-70

Book, *Roy Rogers Cowboy Annual*, British,
 hardcover, 7 x 10 in., 1953 50-65

Book, *Roy Rogers Cowboy Annual*, British,
 hardcover, 7 x 10 in., 1957 35-50

Figure 5-1

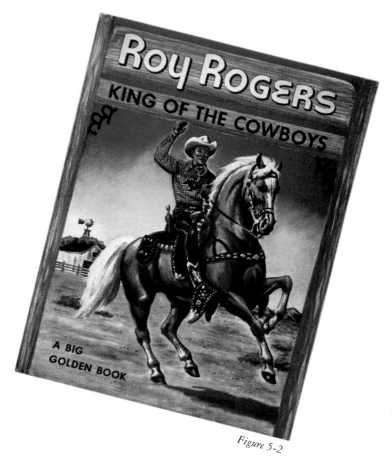

Figure 5-2

Figure 5-3

Book, *Trigger to the Rescue*, photo cover, Cozy
 Corner, 1950s *(figure 5-3)* $15-25

Book, Pop Up, *The Roy Rogers Jump-Up
 Book*, British, Purnell & Sons, 1950s 50-75

Booklet, paper, *The Story of Roy Rogers, King
 of the Cowboys*, B&W, rare, *(figure 5-4)* 35-60

Boot Covers, "Boot-sters," Roy and Trigger, vinyl
 and fabric, box bottom is photo, 1950s 75-150

Camera, Roy and Trigger, metal and plastic,
 4 in., boxed, late 1940s, *(figure 5-5)* 100-200

Card, birthday, Roy and Trigger illustration,
 Waldorf, England, late 1950s 60-80

Coloring Book, "Trigger and Bullet," Whitman,
 1956 35-50

Comic Book Series, *Roy Rogers' Trigger* (Dell Publishing,
1951-55)
 #1 (Dell Four Color 329), painted cover, 1951 . . 50-100

 #2, photo cover, September 1951 30-90

 #3-5, painted covers 12-35

 #6-17, painted covers, title merges with Roy
 Rogers after issue #17 8-25

Comic Book Series, *Roy Rogers*, Dell Publishing
(Becomes *Roy Rogers and Trigger* with issue #92)
 #7, photo cover, 1948 *(figure 5-6)* 30-100

 #23, photo cover, 1949 *(figure 5-7)* 25-85

Comic Book Series, *Roy Rogers and Trigger*, Dell Publishing #128-129, photo covers (*figure 5-8, 9*) $15-35

Cookie Jar, ceramic, 18 in., McMe Prod., ltd. ed. (shown converted to lamp), 1990s 250-350

Crayon Set, Roy Rogers and Trigger, Standard Toykraft, 1950s (*figure 5-10*) 60-90

Direct Mail Ad, fold-out piece on value of training, featuring Trigger, Grit, 1950s (*figure 5-11*) 35-50

Dishes, each piece with Trigger, Rodeo by Universal, center illustration with rope design on edge of plate, 9.5 in., shows Trigger rearing, with Roy on back 50-75

Plate, 6 in., Roy rides Trigger 30-40

Bowl, 7 in., Roy rides Trigger 40-50

Bowl, 5 in., Trigger head portrait 40-50

Figure 5-4

Figure 5-6

Figure 5-7

Figure 5-5

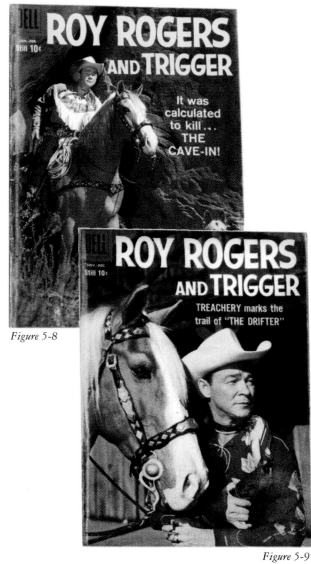

Figure 5-8

Figure 5-9

Figure 5-10

Drapes, made with vintage Roy Rogers fabric . . $100-175

Fan Club Card, with Roy, Dale, Trigger, and
Bullet 30-40

Figures, Trigger and Roy, Trigger stands, Hartland
Plastics, late 1950s, boxed with tag
(*figure 5-12*) 125-250

Figure, Trigger only, loose, standing position,
standard size, Hartland Plastics, 1950s
(*figure 5-13*) 35-50

Figure, Trigger with Roy Rogers, standing,
half-rearing and full-rearing positions,
Hartland 150-250

Figure, Trigger loose, standard size, no
accessories, Hartland 25-40

Figure, Trigger and Toy, small size on card,
Hartland Plastics, late 1950s 60-100

Figure, Trigger and Roy, small size, 4.5 in.,
Hartland Plastics, 1950s 65-85

Flashlight, Roy and Trigger Signal Siren, 7 in.,
1950s 40-65

Game, Roy Rogers Rodeo Game, Dee McCann,
1939 (*figure 5-14*) 100-150

Guitar, Roy and Trigger, 28 in., cardboard and
wood, Range Rhythm Toys, 1950s
(*figure 5-15*) 75-175

Horse Trailer and Jeep, with figures of Trigger,
Roy and Pat, Ideal, 1950s, 15-in. box
(*figure 5-16*) 200-300

House Shoes, Roy and Trigger graphic on side,
child size *(figure 5-17)* $100-150

Lamp, figural, 8.5 in., plaster base, painted,
with cardboard shade, 1950s 150-250

Lunch Box and Thermos, Roy and Dale—Double
R Bar Ranch, wood grain backing, 1953
(figure 5-18) 150-250

Lunch Box and Thermos, "Roy Rogers and Dale
Evans," with all three pets, 1950s 150-250

Lunch Box and Thermos, Trigger, by American
Thermos, 1956 175-300

Magazine, *Jack and Jill*, Trigger and Roy cover
photo, May 1961 20-30

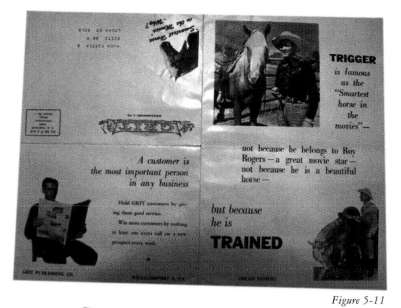

Figure 5-11

Figure 5-12

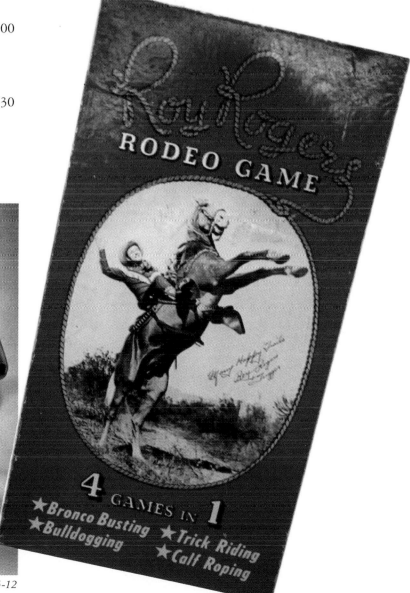

Figure 5-14

Figure 5-13

Magazine, *Life*, cover photo, Trigger rearing with
  Roy on back, July 12, 1943 (*figure 5-19*) $25-40

Magazine, *Listen*, cover photo, January-March
  1952 40-50

Magazine, *Movie Life*, cover photo, January
  1945 40-50

Magazine, *Movie Spotlight*, Vol. 1, #2, October
  1949 (*figure 5-20*) 45-55

Magazine, Screen Stories, Trigger Jr. cover story,
  July 1950 25-35

Movie Poster, *Down Dakota Way*, one-sheet,
  27 x 41 in., 1949 175-225

Movie Poster, *My Pal Trigger*, Republic, 1946 . . . 200-300

Figure 5-15

Figure 5-16

Movie Poster, *Song of Arizona*, Republic, 1940s
(figure 5-21) $200-300

Movie Poster, *Trigger Jr.*, Republic, 1950 100-150

Movie Poster, one sheet, 27 x 41 in., Utah,
Republic Pictures, 1945 250-350

Mug, plastic, several designs, 4 in., 1990s 8-12

Pennant, felt, Roy Rogers and Trigger, 28 in.,
1940s-1950s 50-75

Pillow, made with vintage Roy Rogers fabric to
match bedspread, drapes 35-50

Photo, Dixie Ice Cream premium, Roy Rogers
and Trigger, 8 x 10 in. 50-75

Figure 5-19

Figure 5-17

Figure 5-21

Figure 5-20

Photo, Quaker oats premium, Roy on Trigger, color, 1950s, 8 x 10 in. $25-35

Pin-Back Button, Roy Rogers & Trigger, facing each other, photo, 1950s 15-25

Pin-Back Button, Roy Rogers & Trigger, Roy on left, fringe shirt, bleeds off edge, 1950s 15-25

Pin-Back Button, Roy Rogers & Trigger, Roy on left, fringe shirt, white border, repro 2-5

Pin-Back Button, "Roy • Trigger," drawing, 1950s 10-15

Pin-Back Button, Trigger, head portrait, 1950s . . . 10-15

Plate, ceramic, Singing Cowboy series, McMe Prod., 1995 35-45

Plate, Roy Rogers and Trigger, sepia tone Melmac plastic, M&G Originals, 1986 (figure 5-22) 12-20

Playing Cards, "Happy Trails," Victorville, California, plastic box 8-15

Playset, cardboard foldout, Roy Rogers, Double R Bar Ranch, 1950s 100-175

Playset, Roy Rogers, Double R Bar Ranch, with Trigger figure, 24-in. box, Marx, 1950s 250-350

Playset, Roy Rogers Rodeo, with Trigger figure, 15-in. box, Marx, early 1950s 250-350

Plush Toy, Trigger, 17 in., unlicensed, Brooklyn Doll & Toy Co., 1982 (figure 5-23) 45-75

Figure 5-18

Pocketknife, Roy Rogers' Trigger, with illustration,
3.5 in., Roy Rogers Enterprises, 1993
(figure 5-24) $12-20

Postcards, older black and white, U.S. or foreign,
hard to find *(figure 5-25)* 25-30

Poster, Trigger and Roy, door size, 2 x 5.5 ft,
color, 1957 200-300

Program, rodeo souvenir, Trigger rearing on cover,
"Roy Rogers" on top, 8 x 11 in. 25-35

Program, souvenir program, 9 x 12 in., color
photo on cover, 1950s *(figure 5-26)* 25-35

Pull Toy, musical Roy and Trigger, 8.5 in.,
wood and metal, late 1940s 125-175

Figure 5-22

Figure 5-24

Figure 5-23

Figure 5-26

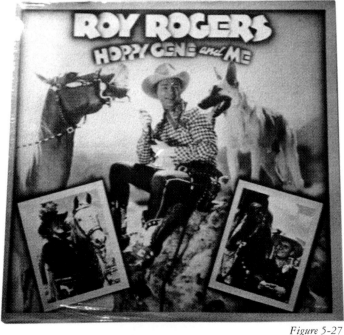

Figure 5-27

Puzzle, frame tray, Roy and Trigger stand
together, Whitman, 1948 . . . . $30-50

Puzzle, frame tray, Roy on Trigger, with cover
photo to frame, 1950 30-55

Record, "Hoppy, Gene and Me" (with Trigger and
Champion), 1990s *(figure 5-27)* 12-20

Record, *Lore of the West*, RCA Victor 30-45

Record Album, Story and Record Set, 21-pg.
book and two 45 rpm records, 1950 50-75

Record Album, *Lore of the West*, RCA Victor
(figure 5-28) 65-75

Record Player, Happy Trails—Roy Rogers and
Trigger, plastic, RCA Victor, 1950s 200-300

Riding Toy, Trigger, plush on metal base with
wheels, 18 in., early 1950s 200-300

Riding Toy, Trigger, skinny in plastic on
metal base with wheels, 18.5 in., 1950s 150-225

Ring, tin lithograph, Trigger, Post Cereal
premium (part of 12-ring set), 1950s 15-25

Scarf, satin, early 1950s, 27 x 27 in., red and
gold 75-100

School Bag, Roy Rogers and Trigger, vinyl with
graphic, long strap, 1950s 75-125

Shirt, plaid with Trigger and Roy on embroidered
yoke, child size, 1950s $75-125

Tin Truck, Trigger's trailer, tin litho 350-450

Trivet, museum souvenir, Plympton's Genuine
Abalone Originals, 5.5 in. across 30-45

Wall Plaque, laminated color photo on wood,
Trigger and Roy, 8.5 x 11 in., 1950s 175-225

Writing Tablet, Roy and Trigger, 10 x 8 in.,
1950s 20-30

Yo-Yo, Roy Rogers and Trigger, with photo on
side, Western Plastics, 1950s 15-25

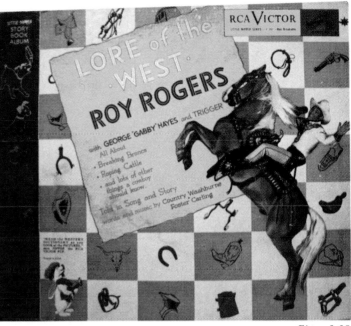

Figure 5-28

Figure 5-25

Flipper

Everyone loves the king of the sea.
Ever so kind and gentle is he.
Tricks he will do when children appear
And how they laugh when he's near!

They call him Flipper, Flipper!
Faster then lightening!
No one you see is smarter than he,
And we know Flipper
Lives in a world full of wonder,
Lying there under . . . under the sea.

Flipper is irresistible. With a smile that just won't quit, he is playful, lovable, and downright heroic. Flipper fans and collectors will tell you he's one of the most intelligent animals around.

Perhaps that is why Flipper has endured more than three decades since his early 1960s film debut, to star in a 1990s syndicated television show and a recent big-budget Universal box office success.

Flipper first appeared in MGM's 1963 film hit, *Flipper*, co-written by Ricou Browning (a former stunt man who actually held the title role in *Creature From the Black Lagoon*). The film starred Chuck Connors as Porter Ricks, and introduced young Luke Halpin in the role of Sandy. A success at the box office, the picture quickly spawned a sequel, *Flipper's New Adventure* (1964), and a weekly television series on NBC.

The 1964 "Fall Preview" issue of *TV Guide* hails the introduction of *Flipper* to television, alongside other notable new shows such as *Gilligan's Island* and *Voyage to the Bottom of the Sea*. Do we detect a trend here? Also interesting is the fact that both write-ups on *Flipper* manage to compare the delphine hero to "a seafaring Lassie," paying homage to the Sunday-night staple then entering its second decade of successful ratings.

Hoping, no doubt, to capture the loyal Lassie viewers with its wet version of Timmy and Lassie, *Flipper* was also aimed at an audience just beginning to appreciate the Beach Boys, *Beach Blanket Bingo* and bikinis. Filmed in Florida, Flipper's sets had plenty of aquatic charm, including white sand, white Keds, a goofy pelican, a miniature submarine, shirt-less guys and bikini-clad gals. *Flipper* was an exciting half-hour Florida vacation, available each week at no charge. Viewers could sit back with a nice cold drink, enjoy the cry of seagulls, and prepare to submerge into the magical world of the dolphin. It was always fun, and always a breath of fresh sea air.

The show starred Luke Halpin, reprising his film role as Sandy Ricks, joined now with Tommy Norden as kid brother Bud, and suave Brian Kelly as their father, Porter. Halpin was elevated to teen heart-throb status during the show's run, although he never dominated the covers of *16* and *Teen Beat* like Sajid Kahn, who co-starred with an elephant named Maya.

Today, Halpin continues to work in the film industry, sometimes in front of the camera, sometimes behind it. He makes frequent guest appearances at collector's shows, and still enjoys swimming with dolphins when he gets the chance. A Florida resident, Halpin has stayed close to his *Flipper* roots, and has, himself, embarked on the adventure of collecting *Flipper* toys and memorabilia.

But, what about the real star of *Flipper*? To be honest, Flipper was played by a series of dolphins. Unlike the casting director for *Lassie*, the *Flipper* crew didn't have to worry about matching the white blaze down the nose. Most dolphins look pretty similar, in the eyes of the television viewing public.

Mitzi was the name of the dolphin who starred in the first *Flipper* movie. The first pupil of dolphin merchant-turned-trainer Milton Santini, she was featured in the January 4, 1964, *Saturday Evening Post*. The article, which featured Mitzi and cover dolphin Suzie, who would star in the *Flipper* television series, touts pet dolphins as "a new status symbol."

The popularity of dolphins has continued to grow since that time, first as pets, then as the smartest mammal, then as metaphysical talismans, then as cancer curers, etc. People love dolphins. And Flipper is still the most famous dolphin of all.

Today, *Flipper* is a perennial re-run favorite. In 1995, a new syndicated *Flipper* series was introduced, and, the following year, a revamped *Flipper* movie starred Elijah Wood as Sandy Ricks, a rebellious 14-year-old city boy forced to spend a summer with his bachelor uncle, Porter, played by Paul Hogan. When the raucous boy and the simple, ex-hippie fisherman get together, everything seems to go wrong, until . . . Flipper comes along.

Three dolphins (and an animatronic one) played Flipper in the 1996 film. The June 1996 issue of *Disney Adventures* features Flipper and Elijah Wood on the cover, and gives a great rundown of the qualities, strengths, and weaknesses of the three animal stars, Fatman, Jake, and MacGuyver. The film's dolphin trainers, Danny Sams, Scott Sharpe, and George "Paka" Nishimura, helped put the information together. In a nutshell, MacGuyver is the best-looking, but the most stubborn; Fatman is playful and easy-going, and Jake is the movie's real star performer.

The 1996 *Flipper* movie, written and directed by Alan Shapiro (*The Crush*), opened in the #3 position nationwide, but had a hard time competing with *Mission: Impossible* and *Twister* ratings. *Flipper* merchandise licensing for the movie was granted to Toy Biz and Applause, both of which introduced a variety of *Flipper* toys.

"*Flipper* is one of those classic properties with appeal to both parents and kids," said Andy Garto, executive vice president of Toy Biz. Toy Biz introduced a clip-on Flipper, which comes with two training hoops that snap together and become a ball. The company also issued 10-inch and 16-inch versions of a plush Flipper that stands on his tail and squeaks "real dolphin noises" when his tail is squeezed.

Toy Biz's battery-operated Swim 'N Splash Flipper came complete with trick toys and a Sandy figure, while the Bubble 'N Squirt Flipper offered a fun twist to the classic bubble blowing toy. The company's Flipper Rescue Set, according to Toy Biz, "lets children learn about empathy and caring as they rescue their favorite dolphin and nurse him back to health. Just hold him in your arms until he feels better, then put him back in the 'ocean' so he can play and perform tricks for you."

Stunt Set Flipper includes a training pole, training ball, water stunt hoop, plush coins and camera with real movie clips. And, finally, Toy Biz rounded out its Flipper line with bean-bag versions of Flipper, Pete the Pelican, and Sam the Turtle.

Flipper toys in the 1996 Applause line included a terrycloth "water buddy" bath toy, two PVC plastic figurines, a plush puppet, a large plush toy, a series of brightly colored, pocket-sized, mini-plush toys, and a plastic figural mug.

The plentiful new wave of *Flipper* toys came as a welcome cornucopia to *Flipper* collectors, who, until recently, have had to look long and hard for items featuring the coveted dolphin. Although the show ran for four seasons (more than 90 episodes), *Flipper* toys have never been in plentiful supply, and production didn't really gear up on *Flipper* merchandise until about 1966, midway in the show's run.

Among the most sought after *Flipper* toys is a model kit, issued by Revell in 1965. The model was actually re-released a few years ago without the *Flipper* nameplate, re-packaged as Darwin, the dolphin mascot of *SeaQuest DSV*.

King Seeley Thermos issued a *Flipper* lunch kit in 1966, and Bandai also jumped on the *Flipper* bandwagon in the mid-1960s, with a battery-operated "Spouting Dolphin" toy.

Mattel produced a "Flipper Flips" board game in 1965, and a *Flipper* jack-in-the-box the following year (which plays "Sailing, sailing, over the bounding main . . . "). Both are valuable and hard to find today.

Gold Key experimented with a short run of *Flipper* comics, publishing a total of three issues between 1966 and 1967. All have photo covers, and continue to escalate in value, according to the *Overstreet Comic Book Price Guide*. Whitman, the most active publisher in the mid-1960s of TV-related paper items, produced a variety of books, coloring books, and puzzles. Among the best finds is a boxed set of four painted frame tray puzzles. Whitman also published one full-sized Flipper hardcover book, and two Big Little Books. The last Big Little Book, *Deep-Sea Photographer*, wasn't issued until 1969, after *Flipper* had left the airwaves. It is harder to find than the other two books.

The Holy Grail of *Flipper* collecting, however, is an extremely rare set of 30 trading cards. A test set, produced by Topps in 1966, it features black and white photos from the *Flipper* TV series. The complete set, in mint condition, is valued at more than $1,000. Individual cards sell for $35 each. No wrapper or box is known to exist.

CONNECTIONS . . .

• *Flipper* creator Ricou Browning was the man inside the monster suit in "*Creature From the Black Lagoon*."

• *Flipper* producer Ivan Tors also brought us *Gentle Ben*, *Daktari*, *Sea Hunt*, and *The Aquanauts*

Flipper Collectibles Price Guide

Bandages, Cardboard box of 25 strips, Kid Care,
1996 *(figure 6-1)* $3-5

Bank, gray plastic, coin slot in mouth, 16 in.,
marked "Flipper TV, © ITF-MGM," 1960s 30-45

Bean Bag Plush Toy, Flipper, 9 in., Toy Biz,
1996 *(figure 6-2)* 4-8

Bean Bag Plush Toy, Pete the Pelican or Sam
the Turtle, Toy Biz, 1996 4-8

Billfold, vinyl with photo & logo insert,
7 in., made in USA, 1960s 12-20

Board Game, "Flipper Flips," Mattel, 1965 55-95

Book, *Flipper—The Mystery of the Black Schooner*,
Whitman authorized TV adventure, 1966
(figure 6-3) 10-5

Book, *Flipper—Killer Whale Trouble*, Whitman
Big Little Book, 1967, color 10-15

Book, *Flipper—Deep-Sea Photographer*, Whitman
Big Little Book, 1969, color 12-20

Book, *Flipper—Junior Novelization,* Price Stern Sloan,
1996 *(figure 6-4)* 3-5

Book, *Fun & Facts All About Flipper*, Price
Stern Sloan, 1996 4-6

Bubble 'N Squirt Flipper, plastic figure with
bubbles, Toy Biz, 1996 5-10

Figure 6-4

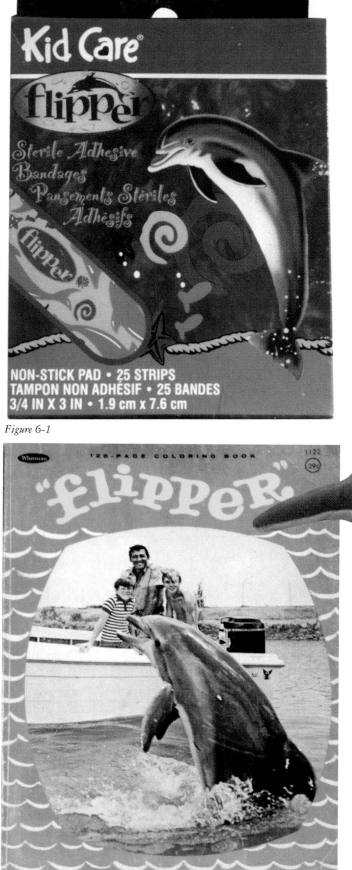

Figure 6-1

Chalkboard, with *Flipper* logo, graphics down
left side, 18 x 24 in., 1960s *(figure 6-5)* $40-65

Clip-on Flipper, carded with training hoops,
6-in. figure, Toy Biz, 1996 *(figure 6-6)* 4-6

Color-by-Number Set, with pencils, boxed, Hasbro,
1966 50-75

Coloring Book, 128 pages, underwater photo
cover with inset photo, Whitman #1122, 1965 . . 15-30

Coloring Book, 128 pages, photo cover with
blue wave border, Whitman #1122, mid-1960s
(figure 6-7) 15-30

Coloring Book, Flipper ringing bell on cover,
Whitman #1091, 1966 *(figure 6-8)* 15-25

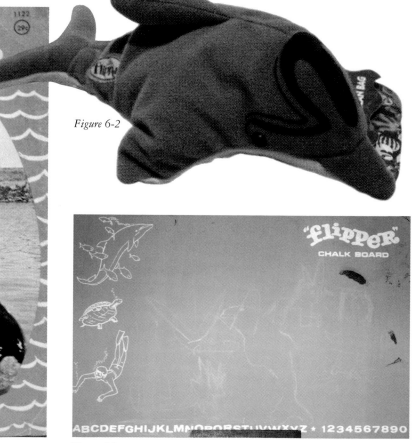

Figure 6-2

Figure 6-7

Figure 6-5

Comic, *Flipper* #1, photo cover, Gold Key,
1966 (*figure 6-9*) $20-40

Comics, *Flipper* #2 and #3, photo covers,
Gold Key, 1966-1967, each (*figure 6-9*) 15-25

Comic, *Flipper*, Top Comics, 1960s, reprint of
earlier Gold Key title 10-18

Cup, plastic, figural Flipper wraparound,
3 in., Applause, 1996 (*figure 6-10*) 5-10

Cup, plastic, Pizza Hut/Pepsi promotion, color
graphic of movie animals, 5 in., 1996 2-4

Cup, white translucent plastic with blue Flipper
design, theater promotion, 1996 2-4

Figure 6-3

Figure 6-24

Figure 6-12

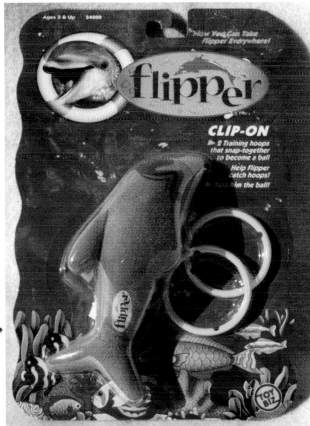

Figure 6-6

Figure 6-8

Disney Adventures magazine, *Flipper* cover story,
June 1996 (*figure 6-11*) $3-5

Figurine, ceramic, "Flipper" on dolphin's side,
6 in. long, Bradley Exclusives sticker, 1960s
(*figure 6-12*) 25-40

Figurine, plastic, Flipper "tail-walking," 3.5 in.,
Applause, 1996 (*figure 6-13*) 3-5

Figurine, plastic, Flipper horizontal on wave,
3.5 in., Applause, 1996 (*figure 6-14*) 3-5

Figurine, waxy plastic, standing on tail, marked
"Flipper" and "Marineland" 25-40

Flip Toy, three variations, Pizza Hut Kids'
Pack promo, 1996, each (*figure 6-15*) 5-8

Flippin' Fun, plastic water game, 6.5 in., Toy Biz,
1996 (*figure 6-16*) 6-12

Figure 6-14

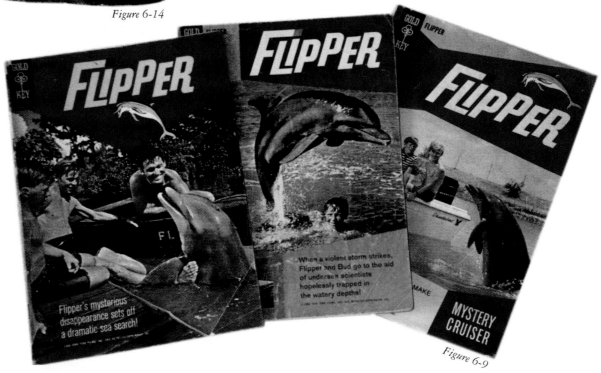

Figure 6-9

Jack-in-the-Box, Flipper in the music box,
Mattel, 1966 *(figure 6-17)* $100-250

Lobby Card, *Flipper*, MGM, 1963 (scene
dependent) *(figure 6-18)* 10-18

Lobby Card, *Flipper's New Adventure*, MGM,
1964 (scene dependent) 8-14

Lunch Box with Thermos, King Seeley Thermos,
1966 *(figure 6-19)* 150-225

Mad Magazine No. 98, Oct. 1965, Flipper
cover with "Flapper" parody *(figure 6-20)* 8-12

Model Kit, Revell, 1965 . . . . 125 175

Movie Poster one sheet, *Flipper*, MGM, 1963 30-50

Movie Poster one sheet, *Flipper's New Adventure*,
MGM, 1964 25-40

Figure 6-15

Figure 6-10

Figure 6-13

Young Luke Halpin comes to the aid of the helpless dolphin.

M-G-M presents "FLIPPER" in Metrocolor

Figure 6-18

Movie Poster one-sheet, *Flipper*, "Finally Safe to Go Back in the Water," 1996 . . . . $15-25

Paint-With-Water Book, photo cover with boys, Whitman no. 1340, 1964 18-25

People Magazine, "Where are they now?" story on Halpin & Norden, July 19, 1993 2-4

Placemat, paper, Pizza Hut squirt puppet promotion (*figure 6-21*) 2-4

Plush Toy, Flipper with sailor suit, 13 in. long, Knickerbocker, 1976 45

Plush Toy, Musical Flipper with sailor suit, Knickerbocker, 1976 40-65

Figure 6-17

Figure 6-16

Plush Toy, Applause, 1996 . . . . $12-20

Plush Toy, 10 in., squeaks, Toy Biz 1996 8-12

Plush Toy, 16 in., squeaks, Toy Biz 1996
(*figure 6-22*) 12-20

Plush Toy, pocket-sized, bright colors, Applause,
1996 3-5

Puppet, Flipper or Scar Hammerhead, squirts
water, 6.5 in., Pizza Hut promotion, 1996 4-7

Puppet, plush, Applause, 1996 15-20

Puppet, soft vinyl, 15 in. long, made in Sri
Lanka for Resaurus Co., 1997 10-15

Figure 6-20

Figure 6-21

Figure 6-11

Figure 6-27

Puppet, Sound Puppet, mouth squeaks, 15 in.
long, Dakin, 1996 . . . . $7-12

Puzzle, 99-piece Big Little Book jigsaw, Flipper
jumping with boat, Whitman, 1967
(*figure 6-23 center*) 12-20

Puzzle, 100-piece jigsaw, photo of Flipper with
Brian Kelly, Whitman, 1965 (*figure 6-23 left*) . . . 12-20

Puzzle, 100-piece jigsaw, Flipper underwater
with Bud, Whitman, 1967 (*figure 6-23 right*) . . . 12-20

Puzzle, large frame tray, Flipper with Bud &
pelican, Whitman, 1966 15-25

Puzzles, boxed set of 4 frame trays,
Whitman, 1966 (*figure 6-24*) 35-50

Figure 6-30

Figure 6-22

Record, "Flipper Theme Song," b/w Anchors
 Aweigh, Golden Records, 45 rpm, 1960s
 (*figure 6-25*) $20-30

Record, *Flipper* movie soundtrack LP, re-issue
 of *Flipper's New Adventure*, MGM 10-15

Record, *Flipper's New Adventure*, soundtrack LP 10-5

Rescue Set, Polyester, Flipper and water stretcher,
 tub toy, 9-in. box, Toy Biz, 1996 8-12

Saturday Evening Post, Flipper cover story,
 January 4-11, 1964 (*figure 6-26*) 12-20

Spouting Dolphin, battery-operated Flipper toy,
 Bandai, mid-1960s 70-100

Standee, cardboard promo for Pizza Hut squirt
 puppets promo, 1996 (*figure 6-27*) 20-30

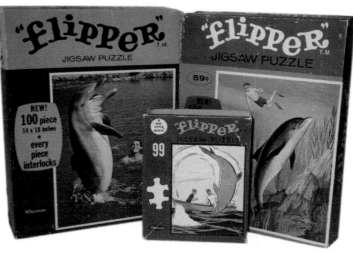

Figure 6-23

Figure 6-29

Figure 6-31

Figure 6-28

Figure 6-19

Figure 6-33

Figure 6-32

Stunt Set, Plush Flipper and accessories in 13-in. box, Toy Biz, 1996 (*figure 6-28*) $15-20

Swim 'N Splash Flipper, 6.5 x 11-in. box, Toy Biz, 1996 (*figure 6-29*) 12-18

T-Shirt, blue tie-dyed with *Flipper* logo, 1996 15-20

Theater Snack Tray and Glass, cardboard & plastic with *Flipper* logo, picture, 1996 4-8

Theater Lobby Display, giant *Flipper* standee, 1996 . . 25-40

Trading Cards, Flipper, Topps test issue, very rare, 30-card set, 1966 900-1,300

Trading Cards, Flipper, Topps test issue, B&W photos, 1966, each card 30-40

Trading Cards, Flipper's Magic Fish, Topps, 10 cards, odd sizes, no gum, each card 8-10

Trading Cards, full set, Donruss, 1996 12-18

Trading Card, Chromium Glitter from 1996 Donruss set, each (*figure 6-30*) 3-5

Trading Card wrapper, Flipper's Magic Fish, Topps, 1966 18-25

Travel Tote, "Fun at the Water," plastic, with toiletries inside, rope tie, 8 in., KidCare, 1996 . . . 5-10

TV Guide, Flipper cover photo, article on Brian Kelly, July 9-15, 1966 (*figure 6-31*) 6-12

TV Guide, Fall Preview—1964-1965 shows, with
  Flipper photo, premier listing, Sept. 19, 1964 . . $30-40

View-Master Packet, "Flipper—Dolphin Love,"
  B485, 1966 *(figure 6-32)* 20-25

View-Master, "Flipper," Talking View-Master set,
  boxed, 1970s 20-30

View-Master Gift Set, "Flipper," 1996, 3-D viewer
  and 3 reels in box, Tyco, 1996 *(figure 6-33)* 8-12

View-Master, "Flipper," 3-reels on blister pack, from
  Paul Hogan film, Tyco, 1996 *(figure 6-34)* 3-6

Watch, Flipper Wet Watch, Kellogg's mail order
  premium, 1996 20-35

Water Buddy, terrycloth Flipper bath toy with
  plastic hoop, 7.5 in., Applause, 1996
  (figure 6-35) 5-10

Figure 6-26

Figure 6-25

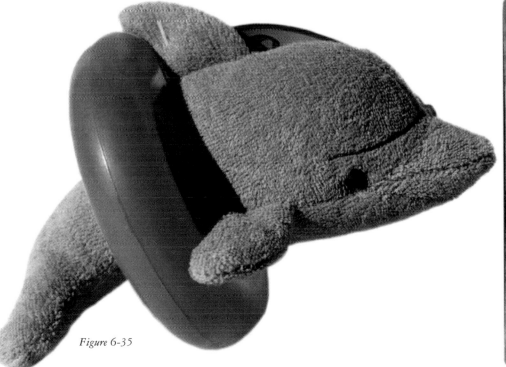

Figure 6-35

Figure 6-34

Benji

"Benji's theme song is 'I Feel Love.' And that is what Benji means to people everywhere."
—Frank Inn, "The Phenomenon of Benji"

Benji was a cute puppy. At six weeks old, his waif-like good looks and expressive eyes prompted an employee of the Burbank Animal Shelter to call Frank Inn. Frank Inn had seen cute puppies before. He'd been a successful animal trainer for about 30 years. He'd worked with Rudd Weatherwax and Lassie, and countless other TV and movie animal stars. But, he agreed to go take a look at the pup in the shelter.

The puppy was a hit, and Frank and his wife, Juanita, adopted the dog and began his education. Of course, at that time, his name wasn't Benji. It was Higgins, and Frank and Juanita were told he was part cocker spaniel, part poodle, and part schnauzer. The puppy learned fast, and Frank trained Higgins at home and in-between takes on the set of *The Beverly Hillbillies*, where Frank was in charge of Elly May's menagerie of "critters." In fact, attentive fans can spot Higgins in an occasional *Hillbillies* cameo.

Hillbillies Producer Paul Henning noticed Higgins, and he was impressed—so impressed, in fact, that he wound up casting the dog as a regular cast member on his new show, *Petticoat Junction*. It was Higgins' big break. He was Uncle Joe's nemesis, and faithful companion to Billy Jo, Betty Jo, and Bobby Jo for seven years, from 1963 until 1970. Usually able to act out his scenes in one take, the dog never had a double or stand-in, and never missed a performance.

Inn said he trained Higgins in 10 to 15 minute spurts, seven or eight times each day, seven days a week. "It's like housework," explains his wife, Juanita. "You never finish . . . "

When *Petticoat Junction* ended its seven-year run, it is widely reported that Higgins went into retirement until meeting Joe Camp and becoming an international superstar. There is, however, one crucial pre-*Benji* film that is too often overlooked. It's called *Mooch Goes to Hollywood*, and was the brainchild of Jim (Mr. Howell) Backus. This 1971 parody features Higgins as an aspiring Hollywood starlet, and treats viewers to more cameos than almost any other film in history. Vincent Price, Phyllis Diller, Jill St. John, Marty Allen, Jim Backus, and James Darren have hefty roles in the film, and the narrator sounds like a Gabor clone. It's quite a departure for Higgins, since the character is female and the content is basically satirical, but the film is quite entertaining and surreal—a must-see video for any Benji fan.

In 1973, Joe Camp had never made a film. He had never worked with animals. But these things didn't stop him from approaching Frank Inn about a new movie idea. The film would be told exclusively from a dog's point of view, and the audience would see and feel things exactly as the dog did. He needed a dog actor—a really good dog actor—that could convey emotion, action, angst, heroism, uncertainty . . . a complete range of emotions and action.

Skeptical but intrigued, Inn was soon won over by Camp's enthusiasm, and agreed to work on the film. When Joe saw Higgins, he knew that was the dog, and Benji's retirement (effective after *Mooch*) came to an abrupt end.

Benji (1974) catapulted the dog to superstardom, and went on to become the third highest grossing film of 1975, bringing in a whopping $30.8 million (just behind *Jaws* and *The Towering Inferno*). Benji was world famous, and traveled the globe, greeting fans, including stops in more than 120 U.S. cities. In 1975, Benji was inducted into the American Humane Association's Animal Actors Hall of Fame at the Patsy Awards Ceremony. The honor, rarely given, had only been bestowed on one other animal—Lassie.

Benji was in high demand, and, interestingly, turned down a lead role (with Don Johnson) in the grim science fiction classic, *A Boy and His Dog*.

Following the success of the *Benji* feature film, the original Benji retired for good, only to be seamlessly replaced by his nearly identical daughter, who starred in a string of films, beginning with *For the Love of Benji* (1977). That sequel, filmed on location in Athens, Greece, was another hit for Joe Camp. The glitzy Hollywood premier of the long-awaited sequel drew such celebrities as Lassie, who presented Benji with a special jeweled collar.

The sequel also inspired a flurry of Benji hype, and the dog was honored with his own ABC TV special, "The Phenomenon of Benji." The TV special, an irresistible zenith of sentimentality and mush, has since been immortalized on videotape and in paperback form. Don't watch it without a handy box of Kleenex.

"Benji is smart," Trainer Frank Inn said in a 1977 interview. "When I first taught the dog to play checkers, I beat it every time. Now, it's only 2 out of 3. This dog and I have more ESP between us than anyone you know."

In 1980, Joe Camp decided to expand Benji's film image a bit. He directed the dog in a somewhat mystical comedy called *Oh, Heavenly Dog!* In the film, co-star Chevy Chase is murdered, and comes back as a dog to track down his killers.

Another somewhat-forgotten Benji appearance came in the 1983-1984 Saturday morning TV season. Benji starred in the only live-action Saturday morning show of the season, *Benji, Zax & the Alien Prince*. The half-hour series saw Benji befriend Prince Yubi (Chris Burton) and his talking robot, Zax, who had escaped their planet and come to earth. Evil aliens provided the excitement here.

By the late 1980s, the phenomenon of Benji had given way to less sentimental trends. *Benji, the Hunted* (1987) was to be Joe Camp's final Benji offering. This film finds "America's Most Huggable Hero" lost and alone in the wilderness of the Pacific Northwest, heroically playing nanny to a group of orphaned cougar cubs.

It's been more than 10 years now since Benji has been seen on the big screen. The year he made his swan song, ironically, is the year that a completely different type of dog superstar grabbed the limelight—Spuds Mackenzie.

> Unlike his noble predecessors, Lassie and Rin Tin Tin, Benji was the first superstar dog to have no breed affiliation—the first mutt to go all the way to the top!

CONNECTIONS . . .
• Benji's owner and trainer, Frank Inn, had worked under Rudd Weatherwax on several *Lassie* projects before discovering Benji.

• Frank Inn also trained Arnold Ziffel, the lovable pig from the *Green Acres* series.

Benji Collectibles Price Guide

Bank, plastic, figural Benji sitting, 10 in., Relic Art Ltd., 1977 . . . . $12-20

Book, *Benji*, movie novelization, paperback with photo cover, 1974 5-8

Book, *Benji, Fastest Dog in the West*, Little Golden Book #165, 1978 *(figure 7-1)* 3-5

Book, *Benji the Detective*, square soft cover, color illustrations, Whitman, 1978 *(figure 7-2)* 3-5

Book, *For the Love of Benji*, novelization by I. F. Love, color photos, soft cover, Bantam, 1977 *(figure 7-3)* 4-8

Book, *The Phenomenon of Benji*, by Frank Inn, 9 x 7.5 in., soft cover, Bantam, 1977 6-10

Book, *The Phenomenon of Benji*, by Frank Inn, small 4.25 x 7 in., soft cover, Bantam, 1978 *(figure 7-4)* 5-8

Book, *Underdog*, by Joe Camp, hardcover with dust jacket *(figure 7-5)* 12-20

Figure, Benji, plastic, Breyer Molding Co. 35-50

Figure, Tiffany, plastic, Breyer Molding Co. 35-50

Figure 7-10

Game, "Benji Game," Waddingtons House of
Games, Canadian, 1976 *(figure 7-6)* $10-15

Lunch Box, plastic, Joe Camp's Benji, with
thermos, King Seeley Thermos, 1974
(figure 7-7) 20-30

Movie Poster, *Benji*, one sheet, 24 x 42 in.,
1974 *(figure 7-8)* 25-35

Movie Poster, *Benji*, one sheet, 24 x 42 in.,
1975 re-release 12-20

Movie Poster, *Benji, The Hunted*, one sheet,
24 x 42 in., 1987 10-15

Movie Poster, *For the Love of Benji*, one sheet,
24 x 42 in., 1977 15-20

Photograph, 8 x 10 in., B&W publicity still
from *Petticoat Junction*, Benji with 3 daughters . . . 5-10

Plate Series, "Wags to Riches," Royal Manor
Porcelain, Creative World Ltd., 1980s

    Benji the Movie Star, ltd. ed. of 19,500, 1982
    (figure 7-9) 20-30

    Benji and Tiffany, ltd. ed. of 19,500, 1982 20-30

    Merry Christmas Benji, ltd. ed. of 19,500,
    1983 20-30

    Benji's Barber Shop Blues, ltd. ed. of 19,500,
    1984 25-35

Figure 7-1

Figure 7-2

Figure 7-3

Figure 7-4

Figure 7-5

Figure 7-11

Plush Toy, Benji sitting, 16 in., with collar and
name tag, Dakin, 1978 . . . . $25-35

Plush Toy, Benji, floppy legs, with collar and
metal name tag, 14 in., Dakin, 1981
(*figure 7-10*) 12-20

Plush Toy, Benji sitting, with collar and plastic
name tag, 9 in., Dakin, 1981 (*figure 7-11*) 10-15

Plush Toy, Benji sitting, 5 in., with collar and
name tag, Dakin, 1978 8-12

Figure 7-6

Plush Toy, Benji standing, 12 in., with collar
and metal name tag, Dakin, 1983 *(figure 7-12)* . . $20-30

Postcard, photo front, back says "Good luck and
Woof!" 3 signatures, 1977 *(figure 7-13, 14)* 2-5

Postcard, Benji at Disneyland, with Goofy and
Pluto, summer 1987 *(figure 7-15)* 2-5

Puzzle, 100-piece jigsaw, boxed, Waddingtons
House of Games, Canadian, 1976
(figure 7-16) 12-20

Puzzle, 200-piece jigsaw, boxed, Benji with rose,
16 x 11 in., Milton Bradley, 1979 10-15

Figure 7-8

Figure 7-9

Figure 7-12

Figure 7-7

Figure 7-16

Puzzle, 200-piece jigsaw, boxed, Benji and
Tiffany, 16 x 11 in., Milton Bradley, 1979
(*figure 7-17*) $10-15

Video, *Benji*, Best Film & Video 10-15

Video, *Benji at Marineland*, Best Film & Video 8-12

Video, *Benji at Work*, Best Film & Video 10-15

Video, *Benji's Life Story* (packaged as bonus on
Hawmps! video), Best Film & Video 10-15

Figure 7-17

Figure 7-15

Video, *Benji's Very Own Christmas Story*, Best
Film & Video $10-15

Video, *For the Love of Benji*, Best Film & Video 10-15

Video, *Mooch Goes to Hollywood*, with star-studded
cast, MNTEX Entertainment, 1970s
(*figure 7-18*) 12-20

Video, *The Phenomenon of Benji*, 30-min. documentary, Best Film & Video, 1979 (*figure 7-19*) . . 8-12

Figure 7-18

Figure 7-19

Figure 7-13

Figure 7-14

Spuds MacKenzie

He was dubbed "the Ayatollah of Party-ola," "the Guru of Good Times," "America's Senior Party Consultant." And, for Bud Light, black and white spokespooch Spuds MacKenzie was pure gold.

Sure, Lassie was compassionate. Rin-Tin-Tin was heroic, and Benji was sensitive. But Spuds was fun.

"He is a jet-set executive constantly surrounded by beautiful women—an enigma, a symbol of all that's fun," touts a 1989 biographical press release issued by Bud Light. "He's known the world over for his smooth style, his sharp wit, his charming and sophisticated ways. He's in constant demand as a guest in the highest social circles."

The bio continues:

To Spuds, having fun is a complex mixture of science and art. And he's the pioneer in the field . . . He's the social virtuoso who can play a crowded room like a Stradivarius.

"I was just born with a talent for having fun," he said in a rare private moment recently. "And I'd be doing it even if I wasn't being paid. The guys who run Bud Light decided it was a talent I should share with the world."

The light-speed rise to Super Star status for Spuds MacKenzie began in 1983, when he met an Anheuser-Busch executive at a party. The executive (who prefers anonymity) was obviously not enjoying himself . . . until he met the 47-pound philosopher.

Spuds shared with that man his thoughts on life and the pursuit of happiness. His words struck a chord with the executive, and he was invited to address a board meeting at the company's St. Louis headquarters.

"Fun is essential to a complete life. And everyone needs to have some at the right times and in a proper way," he told the board. "But in today's world, people get so busy, sometimes they forget how easy it is. Somebody must remind them."

The rest is history. Bud quickly adopted Spuds as a mascot and began spreading his philosophy. Initially, Spuds was featured on posters, then calendars in the mid-1980s. His popularity grew, prompting Bud to test market Spuds on television in California. Big hit!

In January 1987, Spuds MacKenzie made his national television debut during a break in the Superbowl broadcast. He quickly became so popular that by the end of the year, he had starred in 10 commercials, and his image was emblazoned on more than 200 promotional products, including mugs, T-shirts, puzzles, and posters. Spuds was an MTV guest VeeJay in December 1987, and also managed to find time to appear in a film called *Rented Lips* with co-stars Martin Mull and June Lockhart (Lassie's old mom).

By the fall of 1989, Spuds had starred in nearly 20 Bud Light commercials, all of them huge hits with consumers, and all successful at boosting the beer's sales. "When not attending parties, lunching with stars, yachting, or sunbathing, Spuds lives in a lavish condominium at the Anheuser-Busch brewery complex in St. Louis, where he is the 'philosopher of fun in-residence,' according to the Bud bio. "He has a full staff of assistants.

"His other interests include classic films of the 1930s—with 1939 being his favorite year. In literature and music, Spuds' tastes are varied. He often quotes the literary classics, but confesses a love for mysteries. His taste in music covers the spectrum from Mozart to Springsteen. The Beach Boys are a particular favorite."

According to the official Spuds bio sheet, the dog was a "globe-trotting citizen of the world" prior to joining the Bud Light team. His true age was never revealed, as Spuds explained, "Fun knows no age . . . but does have a legal limit."

Bud's official Spuds bio, however, doesn't quite tell the whole story. Spuds, like many screen legends, had a secret past, and a haunting skeleton in his canine closet. Budweiser went to great pains to hide Spuds' dark secret.

Spuds was, in fact, a bitch. Born Honey Tree Evil Eye in the early 1980s, Spuds was known as "Evie" to her owners, Sam and Jackie Oles of North Riverside, Illinois. Budweiser's staff went so far as to shield the dog from cameras when she urinated, to avoid the inevitable scandal and media circus that would follow such an "expose´."

And, while Budweiser managed to dodge that issue, another controversy proved problematic for Spuds. Kids loved him. The dog really couldn't help it. His appeal was universal. Women found him irresistibly adorable. In fact, a beautiful pack of them, known as the Spudettes, followed him everywhere. Men saw Spuds as a role model—fun, popular, cool, and well-traveled. And children loved Spuds because he was a wonderful, funny, friendly dog who loved to play and get dressed up.

Who would have thought Spuds' cuteness could work against him? Mothers Against Drunk Drivers—that's who. And so, as the 1980s drew to a close, so did Spuds' career. He was retired to his Illinois home.

Four years later, in the spring of 1993, Spuds died of kidney failure at age 10. *People* magazine, in its "Requiem for a Party Animal," (10/25/93) recalled Spuds as "one of the most powerful advertising ideas in the last 25 years," and closed with, "Saint Peter, this Spuds for you."

Note: Because Anheuser-Busch cannot copyright a breed of dog, unlicensed Spuds MacKenzie look-alike items flooded the market in the late 1980s. Look for the Bud Light logo on official Spuds collectibles, and make sure the dark patch is over his left eye.

Spuds MacKenzie Collectibles Price Guide

Alarm Clock, Spuds graphic on surfboard, Bud Light logo, round clock, blue base *(figure 8-1)* . . $65-85

Bandanna, red, white, and blue with Spuds graphic, paw print, name 5-8

Bandanna, Spuds graphic, "The Original Party Animal," blue border *(figure 8-2)* 5-8

Belt Buckle, silver metal, Spuds face with logo . . . 20-30

Button, pin-back, photo of Spuds at beer tap, 1987 *(figure 8-3)* 2-4

Button, pin-back, drawing of Spuds seated on logo, in Hawaiian shirt, 1987 *(figure 8-3)* 2-4

Button, pin-back, Spuds on beach chair with umbrella, 1987 *(figure 8-3)* 2-4

Calendar, Spuds photos, pre-1987 20-30

Calendar, Spuds, photos, 1987 or later 10-15

Card "Spuds MacKenzie Card," credit-card style plastic *(figure 8-4)* 5-10

Christmas Ornament, Spuds as reindeer with Bud Light on sleigh 20-30

Coasters, set of 6, plastic & cork on blister pack, Conimar, 1986 *(figure 8-5)* 8-12

Cup, commuter style with wide base, ceramic with Spuds and logo *(figure 8-6)* 12-20

Figure 8-18

110

Cup, ceramic coffee cup, from Opryland,
Nashville, shows Spuds in Hawaiian shirt
(*figure 8-7*) $5-10

Figure, promotional composition statuette,
6.5 in. 70-100

Ice Bucket, with glasses, boxed party set
(*figure 8-8*) 35-50

Key Chain, metal, various designs, each 4-8

Key Chain, plastic, various designs, each 4-8

Lamp, hanging, Tiffany style shade with Spuds
portrait 65-95

Magnet, various designs 2-4

Mug, jar style, clear glass with handle and
Spuds graphic (*figure 8-9*) 8-15

Figure 8-2

Figure 8-3

Figure 8-1

Mug, clear glass, flared top, Spuds graphic
(*figure 8-10*) $6-10

Mug, large size, clear glass, Spuds graphic,
3 designs (*figure 8-11*) 10-18

Mug, standard size, clear glass, Spuds graphic,
3 designs (*figure 8-12*) 5-8

Necklace, ID tag, silver metal with Spuds graphic
and logo (*figure 8-13*) 8-15

Neon Sign, Spuds seated with party hat
& Bud Light 225-275

Neon Sign, Spuds face 200-250

Neon Sign, Spuds with surfboard 225-275

Patch, Spuds with fraternity sweat shirt and
glass of beer 3-5

Figure 8-4

Figure 8-6

Figure 8-9

Patch, Hang Twenty, Spuds surfing $3-5

Patch, Spuds on beach chair with umbrella 3-5

Pen, red with Spuds graphic and logo on white
cap *(figure 8-13)* 3-5

Photo, promotional B&W, 8 x 10 in. with
printed "autograph" 7-10

Pilsner-Style Beer Glasses, set of four shows Spuds
with football and sweater, hard to find
(figure 8-14) 45-65

Pilsner-Style Beer Glasses, Spuds with umbrella or
party hat *(figure 8-15)* 3-6

Pilsner-Style Beer Glasses, Spuds without umbrella,
party hat 5-8

Pin, Hang Twenty, Spuds surfing 3-6

Figure 8-5

Figure 8-7

Figure 8-8

Figure 8-14

Figure 8-10

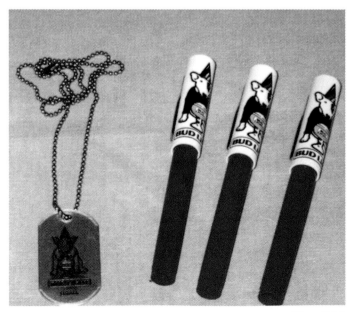

Figure 8-13

Pin, Spuds seated next to surfboard $3-6

Pin, Spuds in white tux, black tie 3-6

Pin, Spuds seated in sweat shirt "Bud Light" 3-6

Pin, cut-out of Spuds in party hat with beer glass . . . 3-6

Pin, cut-out of Spuds seated beside big beer 3-6

Pin, Spuds in party hat with beer in arch design 3-6

Playing Cards, Spuds drawn in white tux with
beer, boxed deck *(figure 8-16)* 10-15

Playing Cards, Spuds photo with guitar
(figure 8-17) 5-10

Plush Toy, Spuds in black tux, red tie, 12 in.,
Applause *(figure 8-18)* 12-20

Figure 8-12

Plush Toy, unlicensed Spuds in Hawaiian shirt,
7 in., Ace Novelty *(figure 8-19)* $5-10

Plush Toy, unlicensed Spuds in Hawaiian shirt,
10.5 in., Ace Novelty 8-12

Plush Toy, unlicensed Spuds in Hawaiian shirt &
sunglasses, 9 in., Ace Novelty 7-10

Plush Toy, giant size unlicensed Spuds in
Hawaiian shirt, 22 in., Ace Novelty 30-40

Plush Toy, Spuds in green suit with logo on hat,
small size 10-15

Plush Toy, Spuds in green suit with logo on hat,
medium size 20-30

Plush Toy, Spuds in green suit with logo on hat,
large size 40-50

Poster, photo (pre-1987) 20-30

Figure 8-16

Figure 8-17

Figure 8-11

Figure 8-15

Figure 8-19

Poster, photo (1987 or later) $10-15

Puzzle, jigsaw, "Rockin' Spuds MacKenzie,"
50-pieces, 18 x 24 in. *(figure 8-20)* 12-20

Salt and Pepper Shakers, five designs, look like
miniature ceramic steins, each *(figure 8-21)* 20-30

Serving Tray, metal, round with Spuds photographs,
"Before" and "After" *(figure 8-22)* 35-50

Sign, Spuds MacKenzie Bud Light Party Zone
("All others will be towed away"), metal
(figure 8-23) 70-95

Stein, light bulb design with Spuds and logo
(figure 8-24) 30-40

Figure 8-23

Figure 8-25

Store Display, cardboard standee, Spuds with
   Spudettes $25-35

Store Display, cardboard standee, Spuds surfing . . . 25-35

Store Display, plastic figural light, 15 in. 150-200

Sweat Shirt (various styles) 20-30

T-Shirt (various styles) 12-20

Toothpick Holder, ceramic mug look 20-30

Watch, four designs, plastic Bud Light band
   and case, Impeneo, 1986 *(figure 8-25)* 40-65

Figure 8-20

Figure 8-22

Figure 8-24

Babe

The world's favorite pig, Babe nearly herded a "Best Picture" Oscar his way. Babe took America by storm, and took the Oscars by surprise in 1996, nominated in seven categories; winning a trophy for "Best Visual Effects;" but missing the highest honor. *Babe* did win Best Comedy Picture at the Golden Globe Awards and Best Picture at the New York Film Critics Circle Awards. Overall, critics declared *Babe* "the best talking pig picture of all time!"

The movie, made in Australia by writer/producer George (*Mad Max*) Miller, cost about $25 million to make; raked in an impressive $250 million; and utilized no less than 800 animals. Babe, himself, was actually played by 48 different pigs, according to an article in the August 21, 1995, issue of *Time*. The problem, of course, was that each pig kept growing out of the role. Veteran animal trainer Karl Lewis Miller and his staff hand-raised 60 piglets, to gain their trust during the shooting. The initial training took 26 weeks, during which time the baby pigs learned quickly, but also grew out of their cutest age phase. Miller was ordered to cut the training time in half, and the piggies were inducted into training at the delicate age of only two weeks.

Each piglet, outfitted with a small hairpiece, was later equipped with a digital mouth on film, and the results were amazing. Babe, and his other animal companions, tell a wonderful story about fighting stereotypes and going for your dreams, as Babe goes to compete in the sheepdog trials.

The movie also comments on the human habit of eating animals, as Babe learns that his family was slaughtered for food, and as some of his other barnyard friends worry about suffering the same fate. This did not stop McDonald's from landing the fast food license for a series of small *Babe* plush toys. Although, more than a few vegetarians were dismayed at the prospect of the chain handing out stuffed *Babe* pigs with its bacon-topped hamburgers . . .

Babe collectibles were, unfortunately, very limited. Movie posters, lobby displays, McDonald's toys, T-shirts, books, pins, and plush toys were offered, although most were in small supply. Hasbro issued a line of adorable stuffed pigs, which promptly sold out and were never re-issued, according to Universal's licensing department.

However, the shortage of *Babe* materials will be a thing of the past soon, as Universal gears up for its *Babe* sequel, expected in theaters by Christmas 1998. That film, tentatively titled *Babe in Metropolis*, features the same creative team as the first, and takes up where the first film left off.

Having triumphed at the National Sheep-Dog Trials, Babe returns home a hero. But, in his enthusiasm to be at the side of his beloved "boss," the little pig accidentally causes a mishap which leaves Farmer Hoggett in traction and confined to bed. With the bank threatening to foreclose, Mrs. Hoggett's only hope for saving the farm is to accept an offer for Babe to demonstrate his sheep-herding abilities at an overseas State Fair in exchange for a generous appearance fee.

Thus, Babe and Mrs. Hoggett set off on a journey that takes them to a far away storybook metropolis, where Babe encounters an incredible assortment of animal friends and learns a few new valuable life lessons.

Universal promises that the new movie, along with a 1998 TV premier of the original film, will spawn a new wave of Babe memorabilia. Already in the works at press time are several lines of infants' and toddlers' clothing and accessories, limited edition prints, candy and snack containers, books, coloring books, mylar balloons, party supplies, posters, calendars, bubble bath and shampoo, school supplies, and more.

Hasbro is producing Babe Playdoh, games and puzzles, while Mattel has plans to release a Babe See 'N Say. Toy Biz is on line to produce Babe Colorforms and kites, and View-Master has plans to release *Babe* products as well.

Schylling Associates Inc. is contracted to produce a Babe "magnetic" dressing doll, a porcelain bank, and tin gift items. Other companies are lined up to produce bedding, curtains, lamps, mirrors, mobiles, towels, statuary, trading cards, Halloween costumes, PVC figures, play sets, sleeping bags, beanbag chairs, and playhouses.

So, collectors who have been frustrated with trying to find *Babe* items, hold onto your hats. They're coming!

Babe Collectibles Price Guide

Bean Bag Toys, Babe, Fly, Maa or Ferdinand,
Gund, 1997, each $5-8

Book, *Babe the Gallant Pig*, by Dick King-
Smith, soft cover, Bullseye Books, 1995 *(figure 9-1)* . 2-4

Book, *The Sheep Pig*, by Dick King-Smith,
original title, released in England, 1983 12-20

McDonald's Plush Toys, all with Babe tag, originally sold
in polybags, 1995

#1 Babe, pink pig, 3 in. tall *(figure 9-2)* 2-3

#2 Cow, black and white, 3.25 in. tall *(figure 9-3)* . . 1-2

#3 Maa, cream-colored sheep, 3 in. tall *(figure 9-4)* . . 1-2

#4 Fly, black and white border collie, 3.75 in tall . . 1-2

#5 Ferdinand, white goose, 4 in. tall 1-2

#6 Dutchess, gray Persian cat, 2.5 in. tall 1-2

#7 Mouse, brown with dark string tail, 3 in., tall . . 1-2

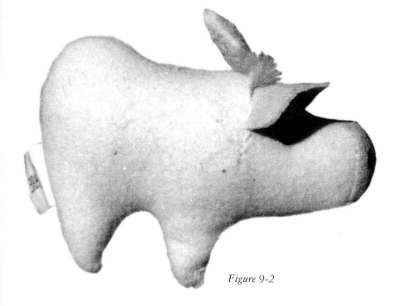

Figure 9-2

Mobile, video promo, Babe & goose on roof, logo
beneath, cardboard & string, 20 in. wide $15-20

Movie Poster, original one-sheet, 27 x 41 in., 1995 . . 25-35

Pin-Back Button, puffy vinyl, Babe cut-out with
logo, video promo, 1995 3-5

Plush Toy, Babe, 10 in., Gund, 1997 *(figure 9-5)* . . 18-22

Plush Toy, Babe, 6 in., Gund, 1997 10-14

Plush Toy, Babe, Playskool/Hasbro, 1995
(figure 9-6) 20-30

Figure 9-1

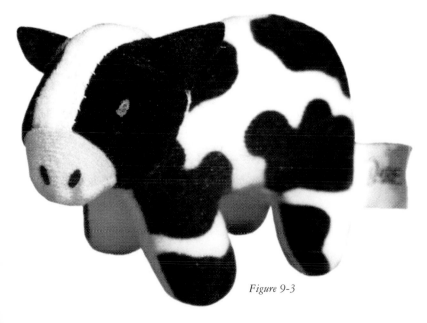

Figure 9-3

Figure 9-6

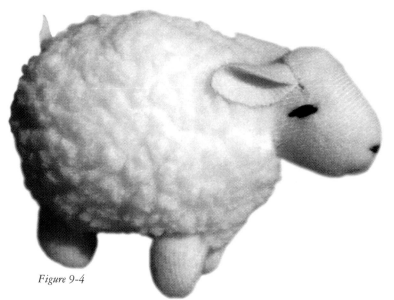

Figure 9-4

Plush Toy, Babe, 9 in., German issue, Playskool/
Hasbro, 1995 *(figure 9-7)* $25-35

Poster, movie poster reproduction, animals with
sunset, 1995 10-15

Puppet, Babe, Gund, 1997 18-24

Standee, video promo, Babe with animals, 60 in.
tall, cardboard *(figure 9-8)* 20-30

Standee, video promo, Babe cut-out, logo on base,
30 in. tall, cardboard *(figure 9-9)* 20-30

Figure 9-9

Figure 9-7

T-Shirt, round picture, Babe with dog and goose,
Hanes, 1995 *(figure 9-10)* $20-30

Talking Plush Babe, Hasbro, 1996 20-26

Talking Plush Babe, Buehler Foods, 1995 25-35

Figure 9-5

Figure 9-8

Figure 9-10

Wishbone

What's the story, Wishbone?
What's this you're dreaming up?
Such big imagination
On such a little pup!

Wishbone is not the first great dog star. There have been several. Rin Tin Tin was brave and heroic; Lassie was compassionate and nurturing; Benji was cuddly and sensitive, and Spuds was . . . well, the guru of good times.

But Wishbone is the first dog star who really loves a good book. Of all the dogs who have ever starred on screen, Wishbone is, by far, the most well-read. (Ask Lassie to recap Poe's "The Purloined Letter" and see how far she gets!)

Wishbone, whose show airs daily on PBS, is portrayed by Soccer, a 15-pound Jack Russell terrier with an incredible tolerance for wearing frilly suits and hats. Owner/Trainer Jackie Kaptan chose the name "Soccer," because the patch over the dog's left eye reminded her of a soccer ball. Coincidentally, soccer balls are among Wishbone's favorite toys.

The brainchild of Rick Duffield, *Wishbone* burst onto the PBS television line-up on October 9, 1995, and has been winning awards ever since. In 1996 and 1997, the Television Critics Association selected *Wishbone* as "Best Children's Show." The show also won a Daytime Emmy Award for Costume Design (1996) and a Peabody Award (1997).

Part of the credit for Wishbone's success goes to his trainer, Jackie Kaptan, who has worked with Soccer for many years. Kaptan adopted the dog in 1988, at the tender age of 8 weeks old, and has been training him ever since. Prior to landing the title role in the *Wishbone* series, Soccer starred in television commercials for Mighty Dog and Chuck Wagon dog foods, and in national print ads, including a photo shoot for Nike. He competed against more than 100 dogs to earn the Wishbone role. This dog knows tricks—lots of them. Among his most impressive stunts are his trademark "WAACKKA!" back flip, and his "sleuth dog" belly crawl.

Following a year-long lapse in production, *Wishbone* entered into his second season in 1997. While the dog looked basically the same, his young human co-stars had aged visibly, now teen idol material rather than just a bunch of neighborhood kids. Wishbone's owners, Joe Talbot (Jordan Wall) and his mother, Ellen (March Chris Wall) are joined in the cast by Joe's best friends, Samantha Kepler (Christine Abbott) and David Barnes (Adam Springfield). Their eccentric neighbor, Wanda Gilmore, is played by Angee Hughes.

Wishbone has become incredibly popular during his relatively brief television tenure. Fans number in the hundreds of thousands, and, appropriately, a Wishbone fan club has been formed. Called, "The Wishbone Zone," the club costs only $10 to join. Fans may also call Wishbone's personal hotline, 1-800-888-WISH , to find out more information on available products, Fan Club information, and TV show updates.

Wishbone Collectibles Price Guide

Action Figure, Robin Hood, 4 in. articulated plastic,
Equity Toys $3-6

Action Figure, Odysseus, 4 in., articulated plastic,
Equity Toys 3-6

Action Figure, Hercules, 4 in., articulated plastic,
Equity Toys 3-6

Action Figure, D'Artagnan, 4 in., articulated plastic,
Equity Toys 3-6

Backpack, plush, 17 x 16.5 in., Equity Toys 18-24

Balloon, mylar, helium-filled, Wishbone's face,
with attached mylar ears 2-5

Balloon, mylar, helium-filled, Wishbone as Romeo . . 2-5

Banner, "Unleash your Imagination," 117 x 8 in. 5-6

Banner, vertical, door size, "Leap into a good book,"
12 x 48 in., 1997 3-5

Banner, vertical, door size, "Follow my lead -
READ," 12 x 48 in., 1997 3-5

Bean Bag Plush Toy, 8 in., Equity Toys 5-8

Figure 10-6

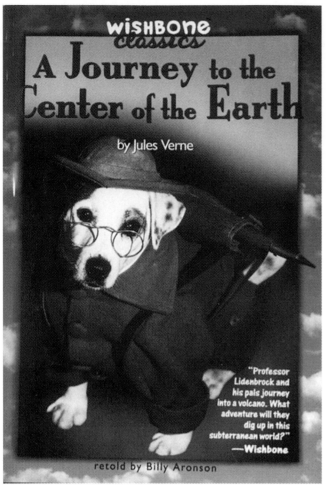

Figure 10-1

Figure 10-4

Book Series, *Wishbone Classics*, Harper Fiction, 1996-97

(All books are soft cover, 7 5/8 x 5 1/4 in., with cover photo of Wishbone in costume and quote.)

Adventures of Robin Hood (The) $3-5

Adventures of Tom Sawyer (The) 3-5

Don Quixote 3-5

Frankenstein 3-5

Ivanhoe 3-5

Joan of Arc 3-5

Journey to the Center of the Earth (figure 10-1) 3-5

Odyssey (The) 3-5

Oliver Twist 3-5

Red Badge of Courage (The) 3-5

Romeo and Juliet 3-5

Strange Case of Dr. Jekyll and Mr. Hyde (The) 3-5

Book Series, *The Adventures of Wishbone*, Big Red Chair Books, 1997

(All books are soft cover, 7 5/8 x 5 1/4 in., with cover photo of Wishbone in costume and quote.)

Be A Wolf! 3-5

Digging Up the Past 3-5

Hunchdog of Notre Dame $3-5

Moby Dog 3-5

The Mutt in the Iron Muzzle 3-5

Muttketeer 3-5

The Prince and the Pooch 3-5

Robinsound Crusoe 3-5

Salty Dog 3-5

A Tale of Two Sitters 3-5

Book Series, *Wishbone Mysteries*, Big Red Chair Books, 1997

(All books are soft cover, 7 5/8 x 5 1/4 in., with cover photo of Wishbone in costume and quote.)

The Haunted Clubhouse 3-5

Riddle of the Wayward Books 3-5

The Stolen Trophy 3-5

Tale of the Missing Mascot 3-5

The Treasure of Skeleton Reef 3-5

Bookmark, cardboard, red and white, fan club
premium *(figure 10-2)* 1-2

Figure 10-3

127

Figure 10-2

Figure 10-5

Bookmark, plastic with tassel, different designs,
Antioch Publishing, 1997 . . . . $1-3

Calendar, 1997, Wishbone—A Classic Hero 20-25

Cap, Wishbone Wear, 1996 10-15

Catalog, *Welcome to the World of Wishbone*,
Hercules picture on front *(figure 10-3)* 2-5

Diary, Romeo photo cover, with keys, Impact Inc.,
1997 *(figure 10-4)* 4-8

Door Knob Hanger, privacy sign, fan club premium,
1995 *(figure 10-5)* 1-2

Jacket, black and khaki, denim, with small
Wishbone logo 125-150

Lunch Box, "Feed the Dog," soft sides, 1996 10-15

Lunch Sack, "Feed the Dog," fabric, 1996 8-12

Newsletter, *Wishbone Zone* Fan Club premium 1-3

Pencils, each 50-1

Photograph, Wishbone with cast, fan club
premium *(figure 10-6)* $5-10

Plush Toy, Wishbone mini-plush, begging, 4 in.,
in chair box, Equity Toys, 1996 5-8

Plush Toy, Wishbone mini-plush, scratching,
4 in., in chair box, Equity Toys, 1996 *(figure 10-7)* . . 5-8

Plush Toy, Wishbone mini-plush, standing,
4 in., in chair box, Equity Toys, 1996 5-8

Plush Toy, Wishbone mini-plush, hiding eyes,
4 in., in chair box, Equity Toys, 1996 5-8

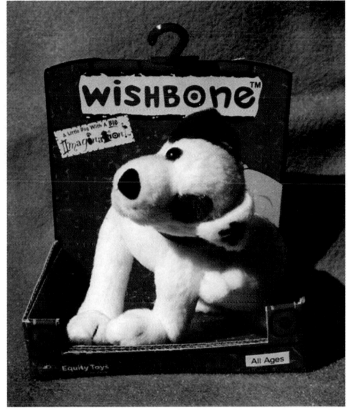

Plush Toy, Wishbone mini-plush, play pose,
4 in., in chair box, Equity Toys, 1996 5-8

Figure 10-7

Plush Toy, Wishbone mini-plush, lying down,
6 in., in chair box, Equity Toys, 1996 *(figure 10-8)* . . 5-8

Plush Toy, Wishbone, sitting, with collar & tag,
12 in., in chair box, Equity Toys, 1996
(figure 10-9) 14-20

Plush Toy, Wishbone in *Sherlock Holmes*
costume, Equity Toys, 1996 19-24

Plush Toy, Wishbone in *Phantom of the
Opera* costume, Equity Toys, 1996 19-24

Figure 10-8

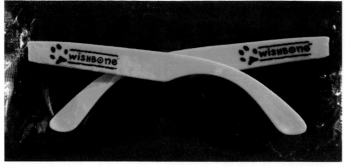

Figure 10-13

Figure 10-11

Plush Toy, Wishbone in *Robin Hood* costume, Equity Toys, 1996 . . . . $19-24

Plush Toy, Wishbone in *Romeo* costume, Equity Toys, 1996 19-24

Postcard, "Prince of Fleas," from Wishbone Zone fan club, 1997 *(figure 10-10)* 1-3

Post-It Notes 1-2

Poster, *Wishbone*, shows half face and profile, 17 x 22 in., 1996 3-5

Poster, *Romeo and Juliet*, 17 x 22 in., 1997 3-5

Poster, *The Odyssey*, 17 x 22 in., 1997 3-5

Poster, *Tom Sawyer*, 17 x 22 in., 1997 3-5

Poster, *Frankenstein*, 17 x 22 in., 1997 3-5

Poster, *Oliver Twist*, 17 x 22 in., 1997 3-5

Poster, *Joan of Arc*, 17 x 22 in., 1997 3-5

Poster, "A Good Book is Like a Good Bone . . . ,"
17 x 22 in., 1997 . . . . $3-5

Poster, "Live the Adventure . . . ,"13.5 x 19 in.,
1997 3-4

Poster, "Leap into Learning," 13.5 x 19 in., 1997 . . . 3-4

Poster, "When You Put Your Best Foot
Forward . . . ," 13.5 x 19 in., 1997 3-4

Poster, "You are the author of your own life
story," 13.5 x 19 in., 1997 3-4

Poster, "To solve a problem . . . ," 13.5 x 19 in.,
1997 3-4

Poster, "Get a clue. Think it through," Wishbone
as Holmes, 13.5 x 19 in., 1997 3-4

Poster, "Listen Up . . . ," 13.5 x 19 in., 1997 3-4

Poster, "Brain Food," 13.5 x 19 in., 1997 3-4

Poster, "Books are a journey into your
imagination," 13.5 x 19 in., 1997 3-4

Shirt, golf shirt, oatmeal color with Wishbone
chest design, 100% cotton 35-45

Figure 10-14

Figure 10-9

Figure 10-15

Figure 10-12

Stickers, with glitter tone, Smello, 1997
(*figure 10-11*) $1-3

Stickers, Hallmark Reward stickers, 8 sheets
per pack, 1996 (*figure 10-12*) 1-3

Storybook Playset, *Prince and the Pauper*,
Equity Toys 9-12

Storybook Playset, *Romeo and Juliet*,
Equity Toys 9-12

Storybook Playset, *Treasure Island*, Equity Toys 9-12

Sunglasses, Fan Club premium (*figure 10-13*) 3-6

Sweat Shirt, *Wishbone* logo, 50% cotton, 50%
polyester 20-25

T-Shirt, "It's a Dog Thing," Wishbone Wear,
1996 12-15

T-Shirt, "Feed the Dog," 100% cotton, 1997 12-15

T-Shirt, *Wishbone* logo, 1997 12-15

Talking Wishbone Plush Toy, 14 in., with collar
& tag, says 12 phrases, Equity Toys, 1996
(*figure 10-14*) 25-35

Tote Bag, canvas $10-15

TV Guide, "Dog Fight," writers clash on Wishbone's
merits, March 15-21, 1997 1-3

Wendy's Toys, originally sold in polybag with
photo card, several styles, 2.5 in., 1996 each
(figure 10-15) 2-4

Video Series
"Bone of Arc" (Joan of Arc) 10-15

"Frankenbone" (Frankenstein) 10-15

"Hercules Unleashed" (Hercules) 10-15

"Homer Sweet Homer" (The Odyssey) 10-15

"The Prince and the Pooch" (The Prince and
the Pauper) 10-15

"Rosie Oh! Rosie Oh!" (Romeo and Juliet) 10-15

"Salty Dog" (Treasure Island) 10-15

"A Tail in Twain" (Tom Sawyer) 10-15

"Terrified Terrier" (Red Badge of Courage) 10-15

"Twisted Tail" (Oliver Twist) 10-15

Figure 10-10

Disney's Animal Stars

Disney films have introduced us to so many animal stars that this chapter will focus only on the major Disney animal stars. Also excluded, but nevertheless wonderful, are Disney's nature documentaries, including *White Wilderness*, *The African Lion*, *Jungle Cat* and others.

During its television tenure, Walt Disney's *Wonderful World of Color* and, later, *The Wonderful World of Disney*, aired dozens of great animal stories. Although most of these short films produced no collectibles, they are still worth mentioning. Among the most notable are *Stormy the Thoroughbred*; *The Pigeon that Worked a Miracle*; *The Wetback Hound*; *The Coyote's Lament*; *Flash the Teenage Otter*; *Chico, the Misunderstood Coyote*; *Sancho the Homing Steer*; *Sammy the Way-Out Seal*; *Little Dog Lost*; *Greta the Misfit Greyhound*; *The Horse with the Flying Tail*; *The Wahoo Bobcat*; *The Ballad of Hector the Stowaway Dog*; *Bristle Face*; *Ida the Offbeat Eagle*; *An Otter in the Family*; *Yellowstone Cubs*; *Minado the Wolverine*; *A Country Coyote Goes Hollywood*; *Concho the Coyote Who Wasn't*; *Joker the Amiable Ocelot*; and *Atta Girl Kelly*.

Disney Films with Animal Stars

Barefoot Executive, The

Big Red

Cat from Outer Space, The

Charlie the Lonesome Cougar

Gordy

Greyfriars Bobby

Gus

Horse in the Gray Flannel Suit, The

Homeward Bound, The Incredible Journey

Homeward Bound II: Lost in San Francisco

Incredible Journey, The

Iron Will

King of the Grizzlies

Legend of Lobo, The

Littlest Outlaw, The

$1,000,000 Duck

Miracle of the White Stallions

Monkey's Uncle, The

Monkeys, Go Home!

Napoleon and Samantha

Nikki, Wild Dog of the North

Old Yeller

101 Dalmatians

Operation Dumbo Drop

Perri

Rascal

Ride a Wild Pony

Savage Sam

Shaggy Dog, The

Shaggy D.A., The

So Dear to My Heart

That Darn Cat

Three Lives of Thomasina, The

Tiger Walks, A

Toby Tyler, or Ten Weeks with the Circus

Tonka

Ugly Daschund, The

White Fang

White Fang 2: Myth of the White Wolf

Disney Animal Star Collectibles Price Guide

Figure 11-1

Figure 11-2

Figure 11-3

Barefoot Executive, The—1971

The Barefoot Executive is about a chimp who can pick the top-rated television shows.

Movie Poster, one sheet $15-25

Big Red—1962

Based on Jim Kjelgaard's classic, this is the story of a champion Irish setter who risks everything for the love of a boy. The title star took home a first place Patsy.

Book, Little Golden Book, D102, 1962 7-10

Comic Book, Gold Key 10026-211, photo cover,
  Nov. 1962 *(figure 11-1)* 10-25

Comic Book, Gold Key 10026-503, photo cover,
  reprints above, March 1965 10-20

Lobby Card, 1962 (scene dependent) 8-12

Movie Poster, one sheet 30-40

Photograph, NBC TV promo for *Wonderful World
  of Disney* airing, 8 x 10 in., B&W, 1964 7-10

Record Set, boxed set of six Disney dog stories 25-45

Soundtrack LP, *The Story of Big Red*, 33 1/3 rpm, photo
  cover, Disneyland Records, 1962 *(figure 11-2)* 8-15

Tomato Box, Big Red tomatoes with graphic,
  Ft. Pierce, FL; no Disney license *(figure 11-3)* 2-5

Cat From Outer Space, The—1978

The Cat from Outer Space stars Patsy winner Amber as "Jake," a clever extraterrestrial feline equipped with a magical high-tech collar. Earthlings help Jake fix his spaceship and avoid capture by the army.

Comic Book, Walt Disney Showcase #46,
  photo cover, Gold Key, 1970s 2-7

Lobby Card, 1978 (scene dependent) 8-12

Movie Poster, one sheet, 1978 20-35

Charlie the Lonesome Cougar—1967
This is a Disney classic, narrated by Rex Allen.

Book, Scholastic paperback, TX 1159, photo
cover *(figure 11-4)* $1-3

Movie Poster, one sheet 20-35

Gordy   1995
This was not the best-received talking pig movie of 1995.
Totally overshadowed by *Babe*, Gordy pales in comparison.

Mail-Order Plush Toy, video offer, 1995 10-15

Movie Poster, one sheet, 1995 10-15

Greyfriars Bobby —1961
Based on a true story, the film is set in 1865 Edinburgh,
Scotland. In the 1940s, Lassie starred in another version of
the story, titled *Challenge to Lassie*. Disney's version stars a
charming and shaggy terrier, who resembles the story's true
life hero much more closely than the famous collie.

Comic Book, Dell Four Color 1189, photo cover,
1961 *(figure 11-5)* 20-60

Lobby Card, 1961 (scene dependent) 5-10

Movie Poster, one sheet 20-35

Record Set, boxed set of six Disney dog stories 25-45

Gus—1976
Gus is a mule who joins an ailing football team as its star
kicker.

Lobby Card, 1976 (scene dependent) *(figure 11-6)* . . . 4-8

Movie Poster, one sheet, 1976 10-15

Figure 11-4

Figure 11-5

Figure 11-6

Figure 11-7

Figure 11-8

Figure 11-9

Horse in the Gray Flannel Suit, The—1968

Dean Jones stars opposite Patsy winner Albarado, the beautiful horse who plays Aspercel, bought to promote a remedy for upset stomachs.

Movie Poster, one sheet $35-50

Homeward Bound—1993

Homeward Bound II: Lost in San Francisco—1995

The 1993 remake of *The Incredible Journey* featured the addition of "thought-voices" for the three lovable animal stars. It was very well received by audiences and critics alike. The sequel, issued two years later, was also a hit.

Bend-Em Figure, Chance, 2 in. tall, carded, Just
    Toys, 1993 5-10

Bend-Em Figure, Sassy, 2 in. tall, carded, Just Toys,
    1993 5-10

Bend-Em Figure, Shadow, 2 in. tall, carded, Just
    Toys, 1993 5-10

Hardee's FunMeal Toys, 1995:

    Chance figure on round base with wheels
    (figure 11-7) 3-4

    Shadow figure on round base with wheels 3-4

    Sassy figure on round base with wheels   3-4

    Riley figure on round base with wheels   3-4

    Delilah figure on round base with wheels 3-4

    Full-Color promotional bag with games
    (figure 11-8) 2-3

Movie Poster, *Homeward Bound*, one sheet,
    1993 20-35

Movie Poster, *Homeward Bound II: Lost in San
    Francisco*, one sheet, 1995 15-20

Pin-Back Button, rectangular video promo, *Homeward
    Bound II: Lost in San Francisco*, 3 1/8 in. 2-4

Standee *Homeward Bound II: Lost in San Francisco*, promo-
    tional display from Video Store *(figure 11-9)* 10-15

(See also The Incredible Journey*)*

Incredible Journey, The—1963

The original version of *The Incredible Journey* features Tao, Bodger and Luath, three wonderful animal stars: Muffy as old "Bodger," Rink as "Luath," and Syn Can as "Tao," the irresistible Siamese cat. Syn Cat also starred as "D.C." in Disney's original *That Darn Cat*, a role for which she won an Oscar.

Lobby Card (scene dependent) *(figure 11-10)* $5-10

Movie Poster, one sheet *(figure 11-11)* 20-35

Record Set, boxed set of six Disney dog stories 25-45

Soundtrack LP, *The Story of an Incredible Journey*, Disneyland Records, 1963 10-15

(See also Homeward Bound*)*

Iron Will—1995

Movie Poster, one sheet 10-15

Plush Toy, Gus, 13 in., with collar, CE, Canasa Trading Corp. *(figure 11-12)* 10-15

King of the Grizzlies—1970

King of the Grizzlies stars Wahb. It's based on Ernest Thomson Seton's *The Biography of a Grizzly*.

Book, Scholastic paperback, 1970s 2-4

Movie Poster, one sheet 12-20

Legend of Lobo, The—1962

The Legend of Lobo traces the life of a wolf from birth to adulthood, showing how and why he avoids humans. Rex Allen narrates.

Comic Book, *The Legend of Lobo*, Gold Key Movie Comics, photo cover, 1963 10-25

Movie Poster, one sheet, 1962 20-30

Movie Poster, one sheet, 1972 re-release 10-15

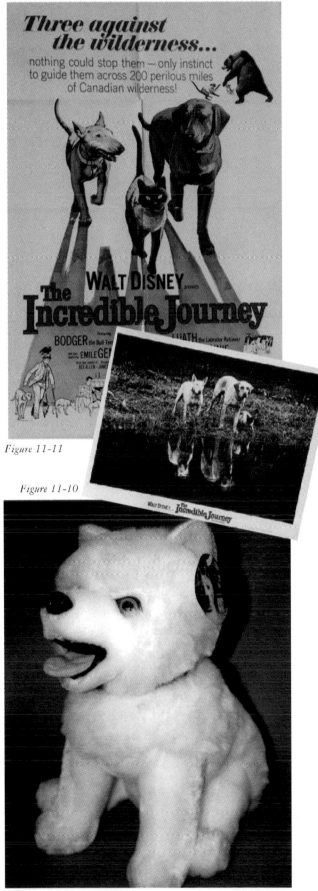

Figure 11-11

Figure 11-10

Figure 11-12

Figure 11-13

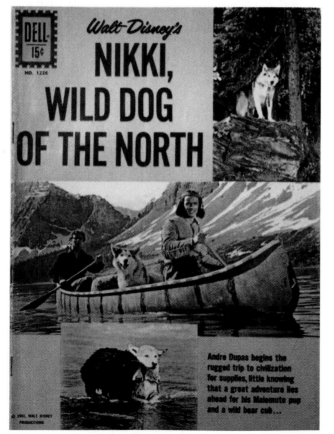

Figure 11-14

Littlest Outlaw, The—1954
Set in Mexico, this one tells the story of an abused horse, set to be killed, who is rescued by a kind little boy.

Comic Book, *The Littlest Outlaw*, photo cover,
　Dell Movie Classic no. 609, 1954 . . . . $8-12

Movie Poster 10-15

Soundtrack LP, *The Littlest Outlaw* (plus 3
　other stories), Mickey Mouse Club Records,
　MM-26 8-12

$1,000,000 Duck—1971
Everyone loves a good duck movie. This one is about a pet duck who lays eggs with a golden yolk.

Book, *Million-Dollar Duck*, Scholastic TX 1939,
　by Vic Crume, with photos, 1971 *(figure 11-13)* . . . 1-3

Comic Book, Walt Disney Showcase #3, photo
　cover, Gold Key, 1970s 4-12

Movie Poster, one sheet 20-30

Miracle of the White Stallions—1963
Miracle of the White Stallions proved to be a rare Disney box office flop, scorned by moviegoers and critics alike. Still, it was a nice showcase for the Lipizzans.

Comic Book, photo cover and back cover pin-up,
　Gold Key, 1963 5-10

Movie Poster, one sheet 15-25

Monkey's Uncle, The—1965
This sequel to Merlin Jones features Patsy winner Judy the chimp (third place) playing the role of Stanley—Tommy Kirk's adopted chimp.

Comic Book, *Merlin Jones as The Monkey's Uncle*,
　photo cover, Gold Key, May 1964 15-40

Movie Poster, one sheet 35-50

Monkeys, Go Home!—1967

Book, Scholastic paperback #TX1055, photos
    on cover, inside, 1967 . . . .$2-4

Movie Poster, one sheet 30-40

Napoleon and Samantha—1972
Napoleon and Samantha are two kids (Johnny Whitaker
and Jodie Foster in her film debut) who run away with a
pet lion.

Comic Book, Walt Disney Showcase #10, photo cover,
    Gold Key, 1970s 4-12

Movie Poster, one sheet, 1972 15-25

Nikki, Wild Dog of the North—1961
Credits go to sled dog Nikki and to Neewa, a grizzly bear
co-star.

Comic Book, Dell Four Color 1226, photo cover,
    1961 (figure 11-14) 10-50

Movie Poster, one sheet 12 20

Record Set, boxed set of six Disney dog stories 25-45

Figure 11-15

Old Yeller—1957
Released on Christmas Day, 1957, *Old Yeller* is one of the
greatest dog movies of all time. It stars Spike, who won a
Patsy for his role (and also appeared in 20th Century Fox's
version of *A Dog of Flanders*). This was Disney's first dog-
and-boy movie, and the best.

Book, Little Golden Book, D65, 1957 10-15

Book, Golden Book, giant-size soft cover, full
    color throughout, 12.5 x 9.5 in., 1958 10-15

Comic Book, Dell Four Color 869, January 1958 . . 15-60

Comic Book, Gold key, photo cover, reprint of
    Dell Four Color 869, January 1966
    (figure 11-15) 5-20

Figure 11-16

Figure 11-17

Figure 11-19

Figure 11-18

Comic Book, Gold Key, Walt Disney Showcase #25, reprints Dell Four Color 869, 1970s $2-8

Lobby Card, 1957 (scene dependent) *(figure 11-16)* . . 8-15

Movie Poster, one sheet, 1957 45-75

Movie Poster, one sheet, 1965 re-release 20-35

Movie Poster, one sheet, 1974 re-release 15-25

Movie Poster, insert, 1957 20-35

Record Set, boxed set of six Disney dog stories 25-45

Soundtrack LP, *Old Yeller*, 33 1/3 rpm, Disneyland Records, WDL-3024 *(figure 11-17)* . . 20-30

Window Card, 1957 25-40

(See also A Dog of Flanders *in Menagerie chapter, which features* Old Yeller *star, Spike)*

Operation Dumbo Drop—1996

Movie Poster, one sheet, 27 x 41 in., elephant painted with army camouflage 5-10

Water Bottle 4-8

Perri—1957

Perri is Disney's second take on a Felix Salten novel, and even features a live action cameo of its predecessor, *Bambi*. Perri tells the biography of a female squirrel, from birth to motherhood, highlighted with wonderful (occasionally gruesome) animal adventures and the message that "to everything there is a season."

Book, Little Golden Book, *Perri and Her Friends*, photo cover, D54, 1956 *(figure 11-18)* 8-12

Movie Poster, one sheet, 1957 35-50

Movie Poster, insert, 1957 *(figure 11-19)* 25-40

Plush Toy, Steiff, 17 cm 75-150

Soundtrack LP, Perri, Disneyland Records, ST-3902 *(figure 11-20)* 10-18

Rascal—1969

Based on Sterling North's classic raccoon novel, this Disney film also features a great performance by young Bill Mumy.

Movie Poster, one sheet $10-15

Ride a Wild Pony—1975

Ride a Wild Pony is set in Australia, where a farm boy and a crippled rich girl compete for the love of a pony.

Movie Poster, one sheet 8-12

Savage Sam (*Old Yeller* sequel)—1963

Based on author Fred Gipson's sequel to *Old Yeller*, Savage Sam tells the story of Yeller's pup, who grows up to fight Indians and protect the family in old Texas. Sam, who looked nothing like his dad, was played by Tom Dooley, who won a first place Patsy Award.

Book, Little Golden Book, D104, 1963 7-10

Lobby Card, 1963 (scene dependent) 5-10

Movie Poster, one sheet (*figure 11-21*) 15-25

Record Set, boxed set of six Disney dog stories 25-45

Shaggy Dog, The—1959

Shaggy D.A.—1976

Based on *The Hound of Florence* by Felix Salten, *The Shaggy Dog* is Disney's third Salten-based film (following *Bambi* and *Perri*). Shaggy, the film's dog star, won a Patsy for his effort, playing the part of Chiffon. He was trained by William R. Koehler, who trained animals for Disney films for 21 years.

Book, Little Golden Book, photo cover, D82,
    1959 8-12

Book, Scholastic paperback #TX1111, photos
    on cover, inside, 1967 2-4

Comic Book, Dell Four Color 985, *The Shaggy Dog
    and the Absent-Minded Professor*, 1959 20-70

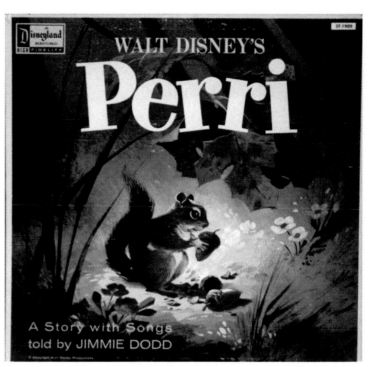

Figure 11-20

Figure 11-21

143

Figure 11-23

Figure 11-22

Figure 11-24

Comic Book, *The Shaggy Dog* and *The Absent-Minded Professor*, Gold Key reprint, 1967 . . . . $10-40

Comic Book, Walt Disney Showcase #46, photo cover, Gold Key, 1970s 2-7

Figurine, ceramic, Shaggy Dog hitchhiking, blue jacket, green base, Enesco, 1959 *(figure 11-22)* . . 40-70

Figurine, ceramic, Shaggy Dog in striped pajamas, brown base, Enesco, 1959 40-70

Figurine, ceramic, Shaggy Dog holds steering wheel, brown base, Enesco, 1959 40-70

Lobby Card, 1959 (scene dependent) *(figure 11-23)* . . 8-15

Movie Poster, one sheet, 1959 45-75

Movie Poster, insert, 1959 *(figure 11-24)* 25-40

Movie Poster, one sheet, 1974 re-release 10-15

Movie Poster, *Shaggy D.A.*, 1976 10-15

Puppet, Gund, red cloth body, white felt hands, soft vinyl head, 9 in., boxed, 1959 25-45

Record LP, *Songs by the Shaggy Dog and His Friends*, Disneyland Records, WDL-1044 12-20

Squeak Toy, soft vinyl, Dell, 1959 20-30

So Dear to My Heart—1949

So Dear to My Heart features black sheep, Danny, sometimes live, sometimes animated.

Book, Little Golden Book, thick size 15-25

Movie Poster, one sheet 120-200

Record Album, with story and pictures, Disneyland Records 10-20

Sheet Music, Lavender Blue, cartoon Danny on cover, 1948 6-10

That Darn Cat—1965 and 1997

The original *That Darn Cat* stars Patsy winner Syn Cat (1st place) who was previously in *The Incredible Journey*.

Comic Book, *That Darn Cat*, Gold Key Movie
Comics, photo cover, February 1966 ....$10-50

Comic Book, Walt Disney Showcase #19, reprint
of above, photo cover, Gold Key, 1970s 4-12

Movie Poster, one sheet, 1965 20-30

Movie Poster, one sheet, 1997 remake 10-15

Press Kit, 1997 remake, color photo folder, 5
B&W stills and press information 8-12

Three Lives of Thomasina, The—1964

The Three Lives of Thomasina is great for lots of reasons. One of its winningest attributes is the scene in Cat Heaven.

Movie Poster, one sheet, 1964 20-35

Movie Poster, insert, 1964 *(figure 11-25)* 15-25

Tiger Walks, A—1964

A Tiger Walks starred Patsy winner Patrina (1st place).

Comic Book, photo cover, Gold Key #10117-406,
1964 10-40

Movie Poster, one sheet 15-25

Toby Tyler, or Ten Weeks with the Circus—1960

Little Kevin Corcoran (of *Old Yeller* fame) stars in this one, alongside Mr. Stubbs, an irresistible chimp. Mr. Stubbs tied for a third place Patsy.

Book, Little Golden Book, (Mr. Stubbs on cover),
D87, 1960 8-12

Book, Toby Tyler, Whitman hardcover, 1960 5-10

Comic Book, Dell Four Color 1092, photo cover .. 20-60

Figure 11-25

Figure 11-26

Comic Book, Gold Key 10142-502, photo cover,
    reprints Dell Four Color 1092, 1965 . . . .$5-20

Movie Poster, one sheet, 1960 (*figure 11-26*) 25-35

Movie Poster, insert, 1960 (*figure 11-27*) 15-20

Playbook, Toby Tyler Circus Playbook, punch
    out characters, Whitman, 1959 50-75

Soundtrack LP, *Story of Toby Tyler in the Circus*,
    Disneyland Records, ST-1904 12-20

Tonka (also aired on TV as *Comanche*)— 1958

Tonka was released on Christmas Day, chronicling the
story of a wild horse captured by Indian brave Sal Mineo.
Tonka is later set free, re-captured, sold to the U.S. cavalry,
renamed Comanche, and becomes the sole survivor of
Custer's last stand. Tonka won a Patsy award.

Book, Little Golden Book, photo cover, D80,
    1959 (*figure 11-28*) 8-12

Book, Golden Press/Whitman, hardcover
    (*figure 11-29*) 10-15

Movie Poster, one sheet 25-35

Figure 11-27

Figure 11-28

Ugly Dachshund, The—1966

The Ugly Dachshund stars Mako as Kenji, the Great Dane raised with a family of dachshunds.

Book, Little Golden Book, D118, 1966 . . . . $10-15

Movie Poster, one sheet *(figure 11-30)* 15-25

White Fang—1991

White Fang 2: Myth of the White Wolf— 1994

The 1991 remake of Jack London's masterpiece is about a great dog living in the dangerous and cold north.

Graphic Novel, *White Fang*, W.D. Publications 3-6

Movie Poster, *White Fang*, one sheet, 1991 10-15

Movie Poster, *WF2: Myth of the White Wolf*,
   one sheet, 1994 10-15

Figure 11-29

Figure 11-30

Western Horse Star Roundup

Horse	Rider
Black Eyed Nellie	Smiley "Frog" Burnette
Black Diamond	Lash LaRue
Black Jack	Allan "Rocky" Lane
Blaze	Jim Bowie
Buttermilk	Dale Evans
Champion	Gene Autry
Cottontail	Gabby Hayes
Diablo	The Cisco Kid
Flash	Tex Ritter
Fritz	William S. Hart
Fury	Joey Newton
Koko	Rex Allen
Pal	Dale Evans' first horse
Pie	Jimmy Stewart
Scout	Tonto
Silver	The Lone Ranger
Silver	Buck Jones
Target	Annie Oakley
Tarzan	Ken Maynard
Tempest	Zorro
Thunder	Wild Bill Elliott
Tombstone	Wyatt Earp
Tony	Tom Mix
Topper	Hopalong Cassidy
Trigger	Roy Rogers
Trigger Jr.	Roy Rogers
White Cloud	Brave Eagle
White Flash	Tex Ritter

Black Eyed Nellie (Smiley "Frog" Burnette)
White horse with black circle painted around left eye.

Dixie Ice Cream picture, 8 x 10 in. color, with
Smiley, scenes from 1941's *Back in the
Saddle* $20-28

Smiley Burnette Fan Club, 5 x 7 in., B&W photo,
with Smiley 12-20

Smiley Burnette Cowboy Song Book (photo
montage on cover) 20-30

Black Diamond (Lash LaRue)
Solid black horse

Magazine, *Lash LaRue Western*, cover photo,
Vol. 1, #7, August 1950 *(figure 12 1)* 20-30

Pocketknife, Lash LaRue's Black Diamond, with
illustration, 3.5 in., no mark, 1993 *(figure 12-2)* . . 12-20

Black Jack (Allan "Rocky" Lane)
Solid black horse

Comic Book, *Rocky Lane's Horse Black Jack*,
Charlton, 1950s, several issues, each 20-50

Dixie Ice Cream Premium Picture, 8 x 10 in.,
color, with Lane, (2 versions) early 1950s 12-20

Figure 12-2

Lobby Card, *Captive of Billy the Kid*, 1951 . . . . . $10-15

Lobby Card, *Gunmen of Abilene*, 1950 10-15

Movie Poster, one sheet, *Bandits of the West*,
   1953 40-75

Movie Poster, one sheet, *Sundown in Santa Fe*,
   1948 40-75

Figure 12-1

Buttermilk (Dale Evans)
Buckskin

When Roy Rogers and Dale Evans began filming their
television show, Dale's movie horse, Pal, was replaced by
Buttermilk, who looked less like Trigger.

Book, *Dale Evans and Buttermilk*, Whitman,
   1956 15-22

Book, *Dale Evans and the Lost Gold Mine*,
   Little Golden Book 213, 1954 10-15

Book, *Dale Evans and the Coyote*, Little
   Golden Book 253, 1956 10-15

Coloring Book, *Dale Evans*, Whitman, 1957 25-40

Figure, Buttermilk standing, with Dale,
   boxed set, 8 in., Hartland, 1950s 125-300

View-Master Reel Packet, "Dale Evans, Queen
   of the West," 1956 25-40

Watch Face shows Buttermilk with Dale, 1951
   (boxed or loose) 75-250

Champion (Gene Autry)

Brown horse with thick white blaze down face, light mane and tail, white socks.

Champion, Gene Autry's Wonder Horse, outdid Trigger and Silver in one respect—while each of the three horses had his own comic book series, Champion was the only one to land his own television series. *The Adventures of Champion* aired on CBS for a half season in 1955-56. It aired opposite *Rin Tin Tin*, and was soon replaced by *My Friend Flicka*.

Book, *Champion the Wonder Horse*, Daily
  Mirror book, British, 1950s $20-30

Book, *Gene Autry and Champion*, Little
  Golden Book #267 *(figure 12-3)* 12-20

Book, *Gene Autry*, Little Golden Book #230
  (figure 12-4) 12-20

Book, *Gene Autry Makes a New Friend*, photo
  cover, Whitman Tell-a-Tale Book *(figure 12-5)* . . 12-20

Book, *Gene Autry and the Golden Stallion*,
  Whitman hardcover 15-25

Book, *Gene Autry and the Badmen of Broken
  Bow*, Whitman hardcover 15-25

Coloring Book, *Gene Autry*, photo cover of
  Champion, Champ Jr. & Rebel, Whitman,
  1952 30-40

Comic Book, *Gene Autry* #97, Dell Publishing,
  March 1955 *(figure 12-6)* 10-20

Comic Book Series, *Gene Autry's Champion*,
Dell Publishing Co., 1950-55

  #1 (Dell Four Color 287), August 1950, photo
    cover 30-80

  #2 (Dell four Color 319), 1951, painted cover . . 10-35

  #3, painted cover 10-35

  #4-19, painted covers, each *(figure 12-7, 9)* 10-30

Figure 12-3

Figure 12-4

Figure 12-5

Figure 12-6

Figure 12-7

Figure 12-8

Drum Set, Bass drum shows Gene on Champion, 19.5 in. diameter, Colmor Co., 1940s $200-300

Guitar, Gene Autry Guitar by Emenee, plastic with relief of Champion, etc., cardboard case (*figure 12-8*) 100-200

Lunch Box & Thermos, Melody Ranch, shows Gene on Champion, steel, Universal 300-350

Magic Slate, Gene Autry's Champion Slate, Lowe Co., 1950s 30-40

Movie Poster, one sheet, *Pack Train*, 1953 125-175

Pocketknife, Gene Autry's Champion, with illustration, 3.5 in., no mark, 1993 (*figure 12-10*) 12-20

Puzzle, frame tray, Gene sits by Champion, Whitman, 1950s 25-35

Puzzle, Champion watches Gene nail up sign, Whitman #2628, 1950s 25-35

Record Album, *Champion*, two 78 rpm records, Columbia, 1950s 20-30

Sheet Music, "Riders in the Sky," with Champion photo on cover, 1949 12-20

Watch, Gene and Champion on face, Wilane Watch Co., 1930s 60-90

Writing Tablet, cover photo of Champion and Gene, two styles, 1950s, each 15-25

Diablo (The Cisco Kid)
Pinto

Coloring Book, photo cover, Doubleday, 1953 . . . $20-30

Coloring Book, Diablo gallops forward with Cisco,
Saalfield, 1954 25-35

Coloring Book, Diablo rears with Cisco, Saalfield,
1950s 25-35

Photograph, 8 x 10 in., B&W promo, Diablo and
Cisco Kid, 1953 10-20

Photograph, Butternut Bread 8 x 10 in., B&W
promo, Diablo rears, "Don't Miss the Cisco
Kid," 1956 15-30

Pin-Back Button, yellow and black, photo of
Diablo and Cisco with show name, 1950s 40-75

Puzzles, jigsaw, boxed set of two,
Saalfield, 10 x 11.5 in., 1951 35-50

Stick Horse, stuffed vinyl head (not pinto),
"Ride 'em Cisco Kid," 40 in., 1950s 40-65

Figure 12-9

Figure 12-10

Fury (Broken Wheel Ranch)
Black horse with small white spot on forehead.

This long-running Saturday morning favorite featured a
gorgeous black stallion, Fury, who lived at the Broken
Wheel Ranch with Joey Newton (Bobby Diamond) and his
adoptive father, Jim Newton (Peter Graves). A total of 114
episodes were made between 1955 and 1960, followed by
network reruns which kept the show going until 1966.
Later, it was syndicated under the title *Brave Stallion*. Fury
was owned and trained by Ralph McCutcheon.

Figure 12-11

Figure 12-13

Figure 12-13

Book, *Fury, Stallion of Broken Wheel Ranch*, 1st
ed. hardcover, John Winston Co., 1959 . . . . $10-15

Book, *Fury, Stallion of Broken Wheel Ranch*,
Grosset & Dunlap #7071, 1971 ed. 2-5

Book, *Fury and the Mustangs*, Grosset & Dunlap
#7072, 1971 edition 2-5

Book, *Fury and the White Mare*, Grosset & Dunlap
#7073, 1971 edition *(figure 12-11)* 2-5

Book, *Fury and the Lone Pine Mystery*, 6 x 8 in.,
Whitman, 1957 (2 covers issued) 10-15

Book, *Fury and the Mystery at Trapper's Hole*,
Whitman hardcover, 1950s *(figure 12-12)* 10-15

Book, *Fury*, Little Golden Book 286, 1957 8-12

Book, *Fury Takes the Jump*, Little Golden
Book 336, 1958 8-12

Book, *Fury*, Whitman Tell-a-Tale, small size 12-20

Coloring Book, *Fury*, Whitman, 1958 15-25

Comic Book, *Fury*, Dell Four Color #781,
March 1957 40-80

Comic Book, *Fury*, Dell Four Color #885, 975,
1031, 1080, 1133, 1172, 1218, 1296 20-50

Comic Book, *Fury #1*, Dell Publishing/Gold
Key #01292-208, 1962 20-40

Comic Book, *Fury*, Gold Key 10020-211,
November 1962 20-50

Comic Book, March of Comics #200 15-30

Puzzle, frame tray, Whitman 15-25

Puzzle, 63-piece Jr. jigsaw, boxed, Fury
   & Joey by fence, Whitman *(figure 12-13)* $12-20

Gypsy
Black horse with white star on forehead.

Gypsy starred with Donna Corcoran, Ward Bond and
Frances Dee in MGM's *Gypsy Colt*.

Comic Book, *Gypsy Colt*, Dell Four Color
   #568, 1954 *(figure 12-14)* 10-20

Window Card, 1954 20-30

Koko (Rex Allen)
Brown horse with wide white blaze down face, white socks
and light mane and tail.

Comic Book, *Rex Allen #14*, Sept./Nov. 1954
   (figure 12-15) 10-40

Comic Book, *Rex Allen #26*, 1957 *(figure 12-16)* . . 10-40

Comic Book, *Rex Allen*, 1950s 10-40

Dixie Ice Cream Picture, 8 x 10 in., several photo
   designs of Rex and Koko, early 1950s, each 12-20

Movie Poster, one sheet, *South Pacific Trail*,
   1953 75-125

Puzzle, from Quaker Cereal box, no. 7, "Silver
   City Bonanza," Rex and Koko, 1951 20-30

Sheet Music, "Rex Allen Arizona Cowboy
   Song Favorites," photo of Koko and Rex, 1954 . . 15-25

Figure 12-14

Figure 12-15

Figure 12-16

Figure 12-17

Silver (Buck Jones)
Solid white horse

Bandanna, Buck Jones and Silver, checkered
 border, 16.5 x 17 in., 1930s $75-125

Book, *Songs of the Western Trails*, music and
 photos, Silver on cover, 9 x 12 in., 1940 25-35

Comic Book, *Buck Jones*, Dell, 1950s

 #1 (Dell Four Color 299), October 1950 30-90

 #2 painted cover, Silver rearing with Buck
  on back, June 1951 15-75

 #3-8, 1952 10-50

Dixie Ice Cream picture, 8 x 10 in., Silver and
 Buck, 1941 25-35

Guitar, wood, graphic of Silver and Buck, "Good
 Luck, Buck Jones & Silver," 37 in., 1930s 100-150

Photograph, 5 x 7 in., B&W promo, "Best Wishes,
 Buck Jones & Silver," 1930s 12-20

Snowfire
White horse

Movie Poster, insert, *Snowfire the Wild White
 Stallion*, 1950s *(figure 12-17)* 30-50

Target (Annie Oakley)
Palomino

Book, *Annie Oakley in the Ghost Town Secret*,
Tagg photo cover, Whitman, 1957 . . . . $10-15

Book, *Annie Oakley Sharpshooter*, Little
Golden Book, 1956 12-20

Book, *Annie Oakley and the Rustlers*, Little
Golden Book 221, 1955 12-20

Coloring Book, *Annie Oakley Roundup Coloring
Book with Lofty and Tagg*, Whitman, 1955 15-25

Comic Book, *Annie Oakley and Tagg*, Dell, 1950s

#1 (Dell Four Color 438) 20-100

#2-3 (Dell Four Color 481 and 575) 15-60

#4-18 (photo covers) 10-55

Comic Book, *Annie Oakley and Tagg #1*, new
series, Gold Key, 1965, photo cover 10-40

Cut-Out Dolls, Annie Oakley with Tagg and
Lofty, Whitman, 1955 40-65

Figure, Target rearing with Annie on back, 9 in.,
Hartland Plastics, 1950s (*figure 12-18*) 50-100

Lunch Box and Thermos, Annie Oakley and
Tagg, steel, Aladdin, 1955 200-275

Puzzle, jigsaw, Target rearing with Annie on back,
Milton Bradley, 1955 (*figure 12-19*) 20-30

Suspenders, Annie Oakley and Tagg, 1950s 25-35

Figure 12-19

Figure 12-18

Figure 12-20

Thunder the Wonder Horse
Black horse

Thunder the Wonder Horse starred with Paint the Killer Stallion and Chief Tonto Thundercloud in Monogram Pictures' *King of the Stallions*.

Movie Poster, half sheet, *King of the Stallions*,
    no year marked *(figure 12-20)* $50-75

Tony (Tom Mix)
Tony the Wonder Horse (Tony Sr.), Tony Jr. and Tony II
Brown horse with white blaze.

Tony the Wonder Horse reportedly understood more than 500 words and could fetch specific objects. He was so popular, Fox starred him in his own film, *Just Tony*, in 1922. Tom Mix bought him in 1909 for $12.50. The Tom Mix museum in Dewey, OK, features a full-size replica of Tony.

Book, *Tom Mix and Tony Jr. in Terror Trail*,
    Whitman Big Little Book, 1934 35-50

Book, *Tony and his Pals*, hardcover, 7 x 8 in.,
    1930s 40-60

Paper Dolls, "Hollywood Dollies," Tom and Tony,
    single sheet, 1925 150-200

Pin-Back Button, Tony's head, name, Ralston
    Straight Shooters, radio premium, 1930s 18-25

Pin-Back Button, Tom Mix and Tony,
    Universal Pictures, red and yellow, 1932 150-200

Pin-Back Button, "Tom Mix and Tony," 1930s . . . 25-50

Riding Toy, "Tom Mix & Tony" wooden horse
    on wheels, 16 in., Mengel Co., 1930s 300-450

Secret Manual, *Tom Mix Ralston Straight Shooter*
    of America, Tony photo cover, 1944 45-65

Topper (Hopalong Cassidy)
White horse

Autograph Book, vinyl cover with zipper,
Topper and Hoppy graphic, 5 x 6 in. $125-175

Bedspread, Topper jumps fence with Hoppy,
100 x 104 in. 175-250

Binoculars, metal, 5.75 in *(figure 12-21)* 75-100

Book, *Hopalong Cassidy and the Bar 20 Cowboy,*
Little Golden Book 147, 1952 15-25

Cap, *Hopalong Cassidy and Topper*, wool
winter cap, Pedigree Sportswear 45-95

Cookie Jar, *Hopalong Cassidy Cookie Barrel,*
11 in., ceramic with saddle lid 125-200

Dishes, set of chinaware with color imprints of
Topper & Hoppy, each piece *(figure 12-22)* 50-75

Dishes, Hoppy's Bar 20 Chow Set, milk glass
plate, bowl and tumbler, boxed 150-250

Domino Set, boxed, Milton Bradley, 1950 150-200

Drinking Glass, white, Hoppy and Topper,
"Healthy Pals!" 3 in. 45-75

Figure, Hoppy and Topper, hard plastic, chain
reins, 5 in., boxed, Ideal, 1950s 125-200

Figure, painted metal, 2 in., made in England ..200-250

Game, Hopalong Cassidy Lasso Game, Topper
figure, graphics, Transogram 125-175

Handkerchief, Hoppy and Topper, 12 x 12 in. ...75-125

Figure 12-21

Inflatable Topper, 19 in. tall, barrel-shaped
body with painted legs, early 1950s $100-150

Lobby Card, *False Paradise*, 1948
(scene dependent) *(figure 12-23)* 50-75

Lunch Box and Thermos, Hoppy riding Topper,
Aladdin, 1954 225-300

Necktie, Hoppy and Topper, child size, 13 in.,
early 1950s 45-75

Pennant, felt, Hopalong Cassidy, shows Hoppy
on Topper *(figure 12-24)* 30-45

Pin-Back Button, "Hopalong Cassidy and
Topper," red, Topper on right, 1950s 15-25

Pin-Back Button, "Hopalong Cassidy and Topper,"
repro of above, Topper on left, 1982 2-5

Pocketknife, black with black and white
portrait of Hoppy on Topper, 1950s 40-70

Pocketknife, Hopalong Cassidy's Topper,
illustration on orange background, 3.5 in.,
1993 *(figure 12-25)* 12-20

Potato Chip Canister, Topper and Hoppy photo
on can, 11.5 in., 1950 *(figure 12-26)* 150-200

Puzzle, frame tray, Hoppy and Topper photo,
Whitman, 1950 20-35

Puzzles, jigsaw, boxed set of 3, Hoppy and Topper,
Milton Bradley, 1950 60-100

Radio, metal with embossed foil, 4.5 in tall,
(high price for Topper with legs up), Arvin
(figure 12-27) 100-300

Figure 12-22

Record Album, *My Horse Topper*, Little Folks
  Favorites, 78 rpm, late 1940s $30-40

Record Album, *Hopalong Cassidy & the Singing
  Bandit*, Capitol Record Reader, 1950
  (figure 12-28) 30-40

Rocking Chair, child size, chrome and vinyl,
  Hoppy and Topper, Comfort Lines, 1950s 100-175

Rocking Horse, Topper, 27 in. tall, plastic
  and wood, Rich Toys, early 1950s 200-250

Scrapbook, vinyl photo cover, Hoppy on Topper,
  10 x 14 in. 100-150

Soap, Hoppy & Topper soap 20-35

Thermos, Hopalong Cassidy standing beside
  Topper, wave design lid, Aladdin, 1950-52
  (figure 12-29) 40-60

Tin Tab Button, Topper in horseshoe, from
  Burry's Hopalong Cassidy Cookies, 1950 20-35

Tin Wind-Up, Hoppy on Topper, rocking base,
  colorful lithographed tin, 11 in., Marx,
  1946 450-750

View-Master Reel, "Hopalong Cassidy and Topper" . . 8-12

Wallet, Hoppy and Topper head shots, black
  with zipper, 1950 40-80

Wallet, Hoppy rides Topper, brown leather
  with zipper, 1950 50-90

Wood Burning Set, 1950 *(figure 12-30)* 100-150

Writing Tablet, with color cover of Topper
  and Hoppy, 8 x 10 in., 1950 20-30

Figure 12-23

Figure 12-25

Figure 12-26

White Cloud (Brave Eagle)
White horse
Brave Eagle, which aired on CBS for a single season in 1955-1956, was unique in the realm of TV westerns because it told stories from the point of view of the American Indian.

Coloring Book, *Brave Eagle*, Whitman, 1955 .....$15-25

Figure, White Cloud with Brave Eagle on back,
    boxed set, Hartland Plastic, 1950s 175-350

Lunch Box, steel, Brave Eagle (White Cloud
    on both sides), American Thermos, 1957 200-300

Playset, Brave Eagle and Horse, 12-pieces, plastic
    figures, Roy Rogers-Frontiers Inc., 1956 100-200

White Flash (Tex Ritter)
White horse

Dixie Ice Cream Picture, 8 x 10 in., color, White
    Flash and Tex, 1938 12-20

Movie Poster, one sheet, *Rhythm of the Rio
    Grande*, 1940 65-125

Photograph, tinted promo still, 5 x 7 in. 12-20

Sheet Music, "Rollin' Plains," photo cover with
    White Flash and Tex, 1937 12-20

Hartland Horse and Rider Figures
figure series (1950s-1960s)

Annie Oakley and Target, with saddle, hat,
and gun, palomino, full rearing $175-275

Blaze with Jim Bowie; brown standing horse,
black mane & tail, white face, legs 150-200

Brave Eagle and White Cloud (black hooves,
standing), 9.5 in., with accessories 200-250

Buffalo Bill with Horse, U.S. Mail saddle, etc.; horse
is brown, white face & socks, semi-rearing . . . 200-300

Buttermilk (buckskin) standing, and Dale
Evans 200-300

Cheyenne, 9 in., Hartland, 1960s, brown, white
face and socks, half-rearing 125-200

Chief Thundercloud with horse and accessories . . 100-150

Cochise (Broken Arrow), B&W pinto, semi-
rearing, with accessories 125-200

Comanche Kid with Horse, 8 in. 60-90

Gil Favor with Horse, 5.5 in., on card 50-85

Jim Hardie with Horse, brown, black mane & tail,
white face, socks, standing, 9.5 in. 75-150

Jim Hardie with Horse, 5.5 in. on card 35-50

Johnny McKay with Horse, 9.5 in. 125-175

Matt Dillon, 9.5 in., standing buckskin horse
(Marshall or Buck), 1960 150-275

Figure 12-24

Figure 12-27

Matt Dillon, 9.5 in., rare semi-rearing buckskin
horse (Marshall or Buck), 1960 . . . . $150-275

Matt Dillon and Horse, 5.5 in., carded 50-85

Maverick, Bret Maverick and horse, brown with
black points, semi-rearing, late 1950s 200-300

Paladin (white with black, Hartland) 7 in.,
half-rearing pose, 1960 150-300

Paladin, small size horse and rider, 4 in., on card
with horse, cowboy and hat, 1960 50-100

Rawhide, Gil Favor with horse, early 1960s 300-400

Rex and Sgt. Preston, black standing horse 150-300

Rifleman, Lucas McCain, and brown standing
horse (black mane and tail), 1960 150-300

Rifleman, 5.5 in. carded version with rider
and hat, 1961 60-100

Scout with Tonto, 9.5 in., standing, Hartland
Plastics, boxed, 1954 . . . . $100-250

Scout with Tonto, 9.5 in., rare semi-rearing
version, Hartland Plastics, boxed, 1954 100-250

Silver with Lone Ranger, 9.5 in. (rearing,
semi-rearing or standing) 200-300

Figure 12-29

The Rebel, Johnny Yuma and brown horse,
small size, carded with rider, hat $75-125

The Rebel, Johnny Yuma with prancing
appaloosa and accessories, 9.5 in. 300-375

Tom Jeffords (Broken Arrow) standing gray
appaloosa Hartland, etc. 250-400

Trigger, palomino with Roy Rogers; standing,
half-rearing and full rearing versions 150-250

Trigger, tan plastic, small version with Roy
Rogers, 4.5 in. 65-85

Wagon Train, Seth Adams and brown standing
horse (white socks), late 1950s 150-250

Wanted—Dead or Alive, Josh Randall and
black standing horse, late 1950s 300-350

Wells Fargo, Jim Hardie and brown half-rearing
horse (white socks), late 1950s 125-250

Wells Fargo, Jim Hardie and brown prancing horse,
dark socks, carded with rider, hat, 1960 60-100

Wyatt Earp and Tombstone, brown standing
horse with rider, boxed or loose 100-250

Wyatt Earp and Tombstone, brown standing
horse, small size, carded with rider, hat 40-80

Figure 12-28

Figure 12-30

Menagerie

Asta

Beethoven

Ben (the bear)

Ben (the rat)

Black Beauty

Black Stallion

Bruce the Ocelot

Budweiser Clydesdales

Bullet

C.J. and other orangutans

Champy

Cheetah

Chinook the Wonder Dog

Clarence the Cross-Eyed Lion
  (and *Daktari*)

Cleo

Cujo

Daisy

Digby

Dobermans

Dog of Flanders

Dunston

Eddie

Elsa

Francis the Talking Mule

Fred

Frogs

Gentle Ben

J. Fred Muggs
  (and Mr. Kokomo)

Joe

Jonathan Livingston Seagull

Keiko (*Free Willy*)

King

Lad, A Dog

Lancelot Link, Secret Chimp

Leo, the MGM Lion

Marquis Chimps

Mister Ed

Misty of Chincoteague
  (and other Chincoteague Ponies)

Morris

National Velvet
  (and International Velvet)

Nipper

Pete the Pup

Rex

Rusty

Skippy the Bush Kangaroo

Strongheart

Tamba the Talented Chimp

Toto

Vance the Talking Pig

White Fury

Willy

Yukon King

Zeus and Roxanne

Miscellaneous and Group Shots

Menagerie Collectibles Price Guide

Asta (Skippy)

The popular and delightfully comic wire-haired fox terrier starred in a string of *Thin Man* films, and later, a different dog portrayed Asta in *The Thin Man* TV shows (1957-1959). The TV Asta won two Patsy Awards.

Asta was originally played by Skippy, a bright pup owned and trained by Henry East. At three months old, Skippy learned to sit up, lie down, speak and come when called. Henry East also trained Jack Weatherwax in the 1930s.

According to one source, William Powell was so smitten with Asta (Skippy), that he offered Henry East a handsome price for the dog, but to no avail. Aside from the *Thin Man* movies, Skippy also starred in *It's a Small World*, *Bringing Up Baby* and *The Awful Truth*, and served as background dressing for a slew of other 1930s movies.

Figure 13-1

Movie Poster, *The Thin Man*, 1934 . . . . . . $7,500-10,000

Movie Poster, *After the Thin Man*, 1936
(with Asta and Mrs. Asta and pups) 1,500-2,000

Movie Poster, *Another Thin Man*, 1939 750-1000

Movie Poster, *Shadow of the Thin Man*,
1941 350-500

Movie Poster, *The Thin Man Goes Home*,
1944 350-500

Plate, *The Thin Man*, Golden Age of
Cinema series, Royal Cornwall, 1979 30-45

Promotional Photo, Asta in center, with human
stars, 8 x 10 in., B&W *(figure 13-1)* 4-8

Figure 13-2

Figure 13-3

Beethoven

Kris, a lovable St. Bernard, starred in two films, *Beethoven* (1992) and *Beethoven's 2nd* (1993). The sequel came complete with a wife, Missy, and a litter of adorable pups. Ironically, the original script called for a different dog breed entirely. Today, it's hard to imagine a Beethoven that isn't a big, drooly St. Bernard. Kris was trained for his role by Karl Lewis Miller, who must keep the sound stage at 60 degrees so Kris won't start panting.

Book, *Beethoven*, paperback novelization with
color photos from film, Berkley Books, 1992
(figure 13-2) $1-3

Book, *Beethoven's 2nd*, paperback novel with
photos, Berkley, 1993 *(figure 13-3)* 1-3

Book, *Beethoven's Puppies*, by R. Tine, new
story, photos, soft cover, Berkley-Boulevard, 1996 . . 2-4

Book, *Beethoven's Puppies' Family Vacation*,
paperback, Berkley-Boulevard, 1996 2-4

Comic Book, Harvey Comics, all issues, each
(figure 13-4) 2-4

Littlest Pet Shop Playset 20-30

Movie Poster, one sheet, 27 x 41 in., *Beethoven*,
1992 15-20

Movie Poster, one sheet, 27 x 41 in., *Beethoven's
2nd*, 1993 15-20

Plush Toy, Beethoven, from *Beethoven's 2nd*, with blue
collar, paper tag, 12 in., boxed, Kenner, 1993
(figure 13-5) 12-20

Plush Toy, Missy, with pink collar and bow
on head, 12 in., boxed, Kenner, 1993 . . . .$12-20

Plush Toy, Tchaikovsky Pup, with red collar, one
paw raised, boxed, Kenner, 1993 12-20

Plush Toy, Mo Pup, sitting with paws up,
boxed, Kenner, 1993 12-20

Plush Toy, Dolly Pup, sitting, with blue
bows on ears, boxed, Kenner, 1993 12-20

Pogs, each 1 2

Stickers, "I Love Beethoven, I love Missy and
the Pups," etc., premiums, 1993, set 1-3

Figure 13-4

Ben (the bear)—Bozo (*Grizzly Adams*)

Not to be confused with Gentle Ben (played by Bruno),
Bozo co-starred as Ben in *The Life and Times of Grizzly
Adams*. He was featured prominently on almost all of the
material produced around the show.

Coloring Book, *Grizzly Adams*, Rand
McNally, 1978 12-20

Game, "Save the Animals," Waddingtons House
of Games, Canadian, 1978 15-25

Lunch Kit, metal dome, 1970s 50-85

Figure 13-5

Figure 13-6

Figure 13-7

Ben (the rat)

This intelligent little black rat took home two Patsy awards in the early 1970s—one for his performance in *Willard*, and one for his title role in its sequel, *Ben*.

Book, *Ben*, by Gilbert Ralston, Bantam
   paperback novel with photo cover, 1972 . . . . $1-3

Book, original hardcover—*The Ratman's Diaries* . . . 10-15

Book, *Willard*, paperback with photo cover 2-4

Movie Poster one sheet, 27 x 41 in.,
   Cinerama, 1972 (*figure 13-6*) 12-20

Record, 45 rpm with photo sleeve, sung by
   Michael Jackson 20-30

Sheet Music, *Ben* theme song 5-10

Black Beauty

Several film versions of *Black Beauty* have been produced over the years, based on Anna Sewell's classic novel told from the perspective of a kindhearted black horse.

Book, *The Story of Black Beauty*, Little Golden
   Book D111 (Disney), Australian 12-20

Figure, Breyer horse 15-30

Figure Set, Breyer horse set (with Ginger and
   MerryLegs) 20-35

Ceramic Figure, limited edition, 6.5 x 8 in. 25-35

Horse Figure, small Warner Bros., 1994
   promotional piece, about 3 in. tall
   (*figure 13-7*) 12-20

Lobby Card, *Courage of Black Beauty*, 1957
(scene dependent) $8-12

Movie Poster, 1921, Vitagraph 800-1,200

Movie Poster, 1933, Monogram 250-400

Movie Poster, 1946, 20th Century Fox
(with picture) 50-80

Movie Poster, *Courage of Black Beauty*, 1957 25-40

Movie Poster, 1971, Paramount (*figure 13-8*) 15-25

Movie Poster, 1994, Warner Brothers 12-20

Figure 13-8

Black Stallion, The

Walter Farley's *Black Stallion* books had thrilled kids and teenagers for decades before the 1979 movie was released, starring Kelly Reno and Mickey Rooney alongside the title character. Four years later, a sequel was released.

Book, *Black Stallion Picture Book*, trade
paperback, color photos, Scholastic, 1979
(*figure 13-9*) 8-12

Figure 13-9

Lobby Card, *The Black Stallion*, 1979
(scene dependent) 6-10

Lobby Card, *The Black Stallion Returns*, 1983
(scene dependent) 6-10

Movie Poster, *The Black Stallion*, 1979 15-25

Movie Poster, *The Black Stallion Returns*,
1983 (*figure 13-10*) 12-20

Figure 13-10

Figure 13-11

Figure 13-13

Bruce the Ocelot (Honey West)

When Anne Francis starred as Honey West in the mid-1960s, her detective mystique was enhanced by the fact that she had the coolest pet on TV—an ocelot named Bruce.

Honey West Pet Set with Ocelot, Gilbert,
    1965 . . . .$65-100

Budweiser Clydesdales

Lamp, Bud Light, with silver Clydesdale,
10 in. high, 1995 *(figure 13-11)* 45-75

Print, framed with logo on bottom,
    cardboard and wood *(figure 13-12)* 50-75

Snow Dome, 4.5 in., Kurt S. Adler Inc., 1988 20-35

Stein, Budweiser Holiday Stein, 7 in., 1988 15-20

Stein, Budweiser Holiday Stein, 7 in., 1989 15-20

Stein, Budweiser Holiday Stein, 7 in., 1990 15-20

Stein, Budweiser Holiday Stein, 7 in., 1991 15-20

Stein, Budweiser Holiday Stein, 7 in., 1992 15-20

Stein, Budweiser Holiday Stein, 7 in., 1993 15-20

Stein, "Snowy Woodland," 6.5 in., Cecamarte,
    Brazil, 1981 *(figure 13-13)* 225-275

Tin, round collectors' tin, (issued yearly) 4-10

Figure 13-12

Bullet (Roy Rogers' German Shepherd)

Bullet starred in the Roy Rogers TV show, alongside Trigger and Buttermilk. He replaced Roy's dog, Spur, who starred in his earlier films. Bullet is now stuffed, alongside his other four-footed co-stars, at the Roy Rogers Museum in Victorville, California.

Book, *Bullet and Trigger—Wild Horse Roundup*,
   Whitman, 1953 . . . .$20-30

Coloring Book, *Trigger and Bullet*,
   Whitman, 1956 35-50

Comic Book, *Roy Rogers #16*, Bullet photo
   cover, Dell Publishing, April 1949
   (figure 13-14) 20-50

Comic Book, *Roy Rogers #25*, Bullet photo
   cover, Dell Publishing, January 1950
   (figure 13-15) 20-50

Figure, Hartland Plastics #700, 6 in., boxed 35-75

Lunch Box, Roy and Dale—Double R Bar Ranch,
   Bullet in center (without thermos) 125-195

Paint-by-Number Bullet and Roy Picture,
   early 1950s (was part of boxed set), loose 10-25

Pin-Back Button, head portrait, "Bullet," 1950s . . 10-15

Ring, Tin Lithograph, Bullet, Post Cereal premium
   (part of 12-ring set), 1950s 15-25

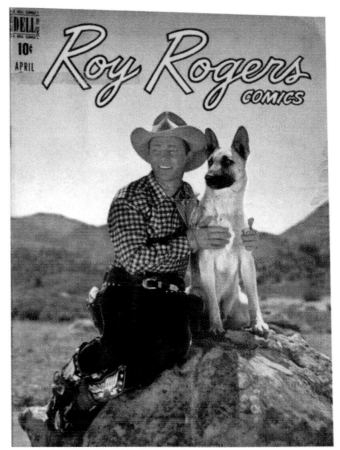

Figure 13-14

Figure 13-15

Figure 13-17

Figure 13-16

Figure 13-18

C.J. (and other orangutans)

C.J. is probably the most famous orangutan star. At his prime—275 pounds in the 1980s—he starred alongside Bo Derek in *Tarzan the Ape Man*, and, as Clyde, with Clint Eastwood in *Any Which Way You Can*. C.J. also had the title role in a short-lived television series called *Mr. Smith*. The show was about an orangutan who has a freak accident and develops an I.Q. high enough to be a lawyer. (There's a joke there, but let's not.) C.J.'s owner/trainer was Ralph Helfer, who also worked with Gentle Ben and the animal cast of *Daktari*.

C.J.

Lobby Card, *Any Which Way You Can*, Warner
  Brothers, 1980 (scene dependent) *(figure 13-16)* . . $5-10

TV *Guide*, cover story, "Mr. Smith," October 22,
  1983 *(figure 13-17)* 4-8

Other Orangutans

Dunston Checks In, advance movie poster, 1990s
  (figure 13-18) 8-15

Lobby Card, *Going Ape*, with Tony Danza,
  Paramount, 1981 (scene dependent)
  (figure 13-19) 5-10

Figure 13-19

Champy

One of the few bovine animal stars, Champy was an angus calf who starred in the forgotten 1961 feature, *Tomboy and the Champ*.

Window Card, *Tomboy and the Champ*, 1961
  (*figure 13-20*) $10-20

Cheetah

Tarzan's faithful simian companion, Cheetah, was a real scene stealer. Portrayed by many chimps since the ape's first appearance alongside Elmo Lincoln's Tarzan in the 1920s, Cheetah has always been a crowd pleaser. He is featured on many Tarzan collectibles.

Action Figure, "Realistic Cheetah," boxed with
  Tarzan, Trendmasters, 1996 (*figure 13-21*) 5-10

Comic Book, *Tarzan of the Apes TV Adventures*,
  photo cover, Gold Key, 1960s (*figure 13-22*) 8-15

Lunch Box, Tarzan, steel, with thermos,
  Aladdin, 1966 70-100

Figure 13-20

Figure 13-21

Figure 13-22

Figure 13-23

Chinook, the Wonder Dog

Chinook was a white German Shepherd who never quite achieved the popularity of his contemporaries, Rin Tin Tin and Lassie.

Lobby Card, *Yukon Gold*, 1952 (scene
dependent) *(figure 13-23)* $8-12

Movie Poster, *Yukon Gold*, 1952 25-35

Clarence the Cross-Eyed Lion (and *Daktari*)

As soon as Clarence opened his eyes as a young cub, trainer Ralph Helfer noticed he was cross-eyed—very cross-eyed. As the young cub grew, it became obvious that he was having trouble judging distances and placement of certain objects, such as door frames, for instance. Helfer called in a special ophthalmologist who created a huge pair of glasses for Clarence to wear. Unfortunately, the only notable effect was that they made the young lion look even goofier than he did on his own.

His vision disability, however, didn't stop Clarence from becoming an animal superstar. In fact, his cute expression, coupled with his loving disposition, landed him a lead role in Ivan Tor's *Daktari* series. Clarence was so popular, in fact, that Tors and Helfer cast him as the star of his own movie, *Clarence the Cross-Eyed Lion*, in 1965. For that film, a vicious lion named Leo, who looked like Clarence (except in the eyes) was used as a stunt double any time a snarl was called for—something Clarence reportedly didn't know how to do.

Clarence's animal co-star, Judy the Chimp, was also enormously popular on *Daktari*. Both animals were trained using Helfer's "affection training techniques," and could be persuaded to do things their natural instincts would never really allow. Judy, for instance, loved playing with Clarence, her natural enemy, and was even taught to hold a snake in one episode. She received more fan mail than any other *Daktari* star.

Figure 13-26

Book, *Daktari—Night of Terror*, Whitman Big
Little Book #2018, 1968 *(figure 13-24)* 8-12

Book, *Daktari—Judy and the Kitten*, Whitman
Tell-A-Tale Book, 1969 *(figure 13-25)* 3-6

Book, *Daktari*, by Jess Shelton, new story based
on series, with photos, Ace paperback, 1966 . . . . . $3-6

Comic Book, *Daktari*, Dell Publishing, 1967-69

#1, photo cover 10-20

#2-4, all photo covers 5-15

Corgi Gift set, die-cast jeep with 5 plastic figures
in 7 in. long box, British, 1973 75-95

Movie Poster, *Clarence the Cross-Eyed Lion*,
27 x 41 in., MGM, 1965 *(figure 13-26)* 25-35

Playset, 140 pieces, with tin litho trading post,
play sheet, figures, etc., Marx, 1967 400-650

Playset, 110 pieces, Marx 1967 300-500

TV Guide, cover story, "Clarence," August 6,
1966 *(figure 13-27)* 8-12

TV Guide, cover story, "Ivan Tors trainer with
tigers at Daktari set," June 22-28, 1968 4-8

View-Master Reel Set, *Daktari*, packet with 3
reels and booklet, GAF, 1968 20-30

Cleo (The People's Choice)

This lovable basset hound was the first TV dog to "voice"
its thoughts. Cleo was trained by Frank Inn, who would
later become one of the world's best known animal trainers, alongside his dog, Benji.

Book, Little Golden Book, "Cleo," photo cover,
#287, 1957 6-10

Figure 13-24

Figure 13-25

Figure 13-27

Cujo

Stephen King's idea of a dog movie, *Cujo* featured a slobbering, rabid St. Bernard on a rampage. Move over, Old Yeller. And, collectors needn't waste any time looking for the *Cujo* stuffed animals . . .

Movie Poster, one sheet, 27 x 41 in., 1983 . . . . . . $15-25

Daisy (*Blondie* movie series)

In the 1940s, the successful series of *Blondie* films featured a shaggy little terrier as Daisy, the Bumstead's loyal but mischievous house pet. Daisy was immensely popular, stealing many a scene from Penny Singleton and Arthur Lake. She was prominently featured on many of the posters and promotional items for the film series.

Lobby Card, *Life with Blondie*, Columbia
    Pictures, 1945 (scene dependent) 15-25

Movie Poster, one sheet, *Blondie's Reward*,
    Columbia Pictures, 1948 (*figure 13-28*) 50-75

Movie Poster, insert, *Blondie for Victory*,
    Columbia Pictures, 1942 (*figure 13-29*) 40-65

Figure 13-28

Figure 13-29

Digby

In 1974, *Digby—The Biggest Dog in the World* was released, starring a lovable Old English Sheepdog in the title role, as a Godzilla-sized pooch who is pursued by scientists and crooks.

Movie Poster, one sheet, 1974 (*figure 13-30*) 8-12

Figure 13-30

Dobermans

The early 1970s spawned a new kind of dog star—the killer Doberman pinscher. No less than three feature films were made, featuring vicious Dobermans.

Movie Poster, one sheet, *The Doberman Gang*, 1972 *(figure 13-31)* $12-20

Movie Poster, one sheet, *Those Amazing Dobermans*, 1976 12-20

Movie Poster, one sheet, *They Only Kill Their Masters*, MGM, 1972 *(figure 13-32)* 15-25

Dog of Flanders

In 1935, a beautiful German Shepherd named "Lightning" starred in the first film version of *A Dog of Flanders*. Lightning was the grandson of Stronghcart, the first great dog star, and had apparently inherited his grandfather's incredible intelligence and star quality. Often requiring only one take to complete a scene, Lightning also starred as a seeing eye dog opposite Cary Grant and Myrna Loy in *Wings in the Dark*.

Another major dog star was featured in the 1960 version of the story, produced by 20th Century Fox. Spike, star of *Old Yeller*, took on the role, and handled it with flair.

Comic Book, Dell Four Color #1088, March 1960 *(figure 13-33)* 25-45

Poster, 1935 RKO 75-125

Poster, 1960 20th Century Fox 10-15

Dunston
(see C.J.—and Other Orangutans, above)

Figure 13-31

Figure 13-32

Figure 13-33

Figure 13-34

Eddie (*Frasier*)

The lovable dog owned by Frasier Crane's father on the hit comedy, *Frasier*, is portrayed by Moose, a Jack Russell terrier. According to *TV Guide*, the dog receives about 10 fan letters each week. He was introduced to acting after his original owners gave him to trainer Mathilde de Cagney. It seems Moose had destroyed their house.

Calendar, Eddie Calendar, 1995 . . . .$8-12

Cap, baseball style, Eddie on front 10-15

T-Shirt, photo with Eddie's name underneath 15-20

TV Guide, cover photo (with Murray from
Mad About You), June 18, 1994 *(figure 13-34)* 3-5

Elsa (*Born Free*, 1966, and *Living Free*, 1972)

Based on the real life adventures of Elsa the lioness, *Born Free* tells of how she was found as an orphan cub by George Adamson, a Kenya game warden, and his wife, Joy, who would later make Elsa famous in her books. The Adamsons raise Elsa, only to decide that she must return to the wild. So, they begin the trying and risky task of teaching a lion how to live in the wild.

The film version of *Born Free* (1966) won two Academy Awards.

In the first sequel, *Living Free*, Elsa's transition to life on the wild side has been completed admirably, and she is back to visit the Adamson's with three cubs of her own. After Elsa contracts a virus and dies, however, the cubs get into trouble and must be relocated to a large game preserve 700 miles away.

Joy Adamson also wrote a third Elsa book, *Forever Free*, which was never put on film.

Book, *Living Free*, by Joy Adamson, Scholastic
soft cover, abridged with photos, 1960s 2-4

Lobby Card, *Born Free*, 1966 (scene dependent)
(figure 13-35, 36) 8-12

Figure 13-35

Movie Poster, *Born Free*, one sheet, 27 x 41 in.,
    1966 . . . . $35-50

Movie Poster, *Living Free*, one sheet, 27 x 41 in.,
    1972 15-25

Record LP, *Living Free • Born Free*, book
    inside, 33 1/3 rpm, Disneyland Records, 1972 . . 10-16

Record LP, *Born Free*, Andy Williams, 1960s 3-5

Sheet Music, "Born Free," by John Barry &
    Don Black, 1966 4-8

Figure 13 36

Francis the Talking Mule

Universal introduced the character in the 1950s film,
Francis the Talking Mule. With co-star Donald O'Connor,
Francis made six movies, and a seventh with Mickey
Rooney in 1955. Although Francis was reportedly pur-
chased for a mere $350, the mule made millions. But, his
life was not all luxurious stardom. Once, Francis managed
to gain 250 pounds between films, and was ordered to
drop them—in just a few weeks. With a strict diet and
grueling exercise, the mule dropped 200 pounds by dead-
line, and was okayed to star in the film. Chill Wills provided the voice of Francis. In 1951, Francis was awarded
the very first Patsy Award.

Comic Book, *Francis, The Famous Talking Mule*, all in Dell
Four Color Series
    #335 30-80

    #465 20-50

    #501, 547, 579 15-40

    #621, 655, 698, 710, 745, 810, 863, 906, 953,
      991, 1068, 1090 10-30

Lobby Card, *Francis Covers the Big Town*,
    1952 (scene dependent) 10-15

Figure 13-39

Figure 13-38

Figure 13-37

Figure 13-40

Movie Poster, one sheet, *Francis the Talking Mule*, 1949-50 . . . . $120-200

Movie Poster, one sheet, *Francis Goes to the Races*, 1951 60-100

Movie Poster, one sheet, *Francis Goes to West Point*, 1952 50-85

Movie Poster, insert, *Francis Goes to West Point*, 1952 *(figure 13-37)* 30-55

Movie Poster, one sheet, *Francis Covers the Big Town*, 1952 *(figure 13-38)* 50-85

Movie Poster, one sheet, *Francis Joins the Wacs*, 1954 40-70

Movie Poster, one sheet, *Francis in the Navy*, 1955 50-85

Movie Poster, one sheet, *Francis in the Haunted House* (Mickey Rooney), 1955 *(figure 13-39)* 40-70

Pin-Back Button, "I Like Francis," yellow metal litho, 1950s 15-25

Fred
Baretta's smart and beautiful Cockatoo was one of TV's most successful bird stars.

TV Guide, cover story, Dec. 27, 1975 *(figure 13-40)* 6-10

Frogs

This Ray Milland thriller may be the zenith of the "Nature Strikes Back" movie fad of the 1970s. Featuring hundreds of amphibian stars, it remains a true classic.

Ad Slick for Newspapers, 1972 *(figure 13-41)* $2-5

Movie Poster, one sheet, 1972 30-45

Figure 13-41

Gentle Ben

Ivan Tors, creator of *Flipper*, continued his success with animal stars by launching the *Gentle Ben* series (also filmed in Florida). The series, included in CBS's 1967-1968 and 1968-1969 seasons, starred Bruno as Gentle Ben and little Clint Howard (Ron's brother) as Mark Wedloe. Dennis Weaver was dad.

Bruno had been born in Canada, where bears typically grow larger than their southern relatives. He stood more than eight feet tall and weighed 630 pounds.

The series was introduced following the 1967 feature film, *Gentle Giant*, based on Walt Morley's novel, *Gentle Ben*. The movie version featured the same cast as the television series.

Book, *Gentle Ben*, by Walt Morcy, hardback,
Dutton, 1965 (1974 printing shown)
(figure 13-42) 4-8

Book, *Gentle Ben and the Pesky Puppy*,
Whitman Tell-A-Tale Book, 1969 3-6

Comic Book, *Gentle Ben*, Dell Publishing, #1,
photo cover, 1968 10-25

Comic Book, *Gentle Ben*, Dell Publishing, #2-5,
all photo covers, 1968-69 5-15

Game, Gentle Ben Animal Hunt Game,
Mattel, 1967 25-40

Figure 13-42

Figure 13-45

Figure 13-43

Lunch Box, with thermos, Aladdin, 1968
(figure 13-43) $75-100

Movie Poster, *Gentle Giant*, Paramount, 1967 12-20

Plush Toy, sawdust stuffed, unlicensed, black
bear with red plastic collar and leash, 1960 10-15

TV Guide, cover story, August 10-16, 1968
(figure 13-44) 4-8

Talking Plush Toy, 16 in., with "Hero"
medallion, Mattel, 1967 *(figure 13-45)* 30-45

Figure 13-44

J. Fred Muggs (and Mr. Kokomo)

In the mid-1950s, ratings for NBC's *Today Show* were
floundering. Producers felt the show needed an extra spark,
and someone came up with idea to introduce a chimpanzee
to the line-up. J. Fred Muggs was an instant hit, and
became a huge star during his four-year tenure on the show.
The chimp salvaged the show's ratings and made personal
appearances around the country. Plush toys, hand puppets,
and books were produced featuring the chimp. Items are
usually marked "National Broadcasting Co."

Book, Little Golden Book, *J. Fred Muggs*,
#234, 1955 *(figure 13-46)* 10-15

Magazine, *Jack and Jill*, article—"Meet TV's
Kokomo, Jr.," April 1961 3-5

Pin-Back Button, photo, "Get Ahead with
J. Fred," black & white, 1950s 10-15

Plush toy, rubber head, yellow pants, striped
shirt, 14 in. tall, with box/chair,
Ideal, 1955 100-150

Puppet, cloth body, soft rubber head, 9 in. tall,
1950s 20-35

Joe ("Run, Joe, Run")

The live action Saturday morning show ran from 1974-1976, with a plot line which seemed to combine *Lassie Come Home* and *The Fugitive*. Joe, a German Shepherd in training at the Army K-9 corps, is falsely accused of attacking his master. As he runs from his pursuers, Joe manages to help those in need on a weekly basis. The title character was ably acted by Heinrich of Midvale.

Action Figure, Joe $18-30

Action Figure, Buck 18-30

Jonathan Livingston Seagull

Based on Richard Bach's inspirational best-selling book, the *Jonathan Livingston Seagull* movie (1973) did not fare as well with critics or the general public. Voices were provided by James Franciscus and Juliet Mills.

Game, the "Jonathan Livingston Seagull Game of
  Individual Challenge" *(figure 13-47)* 25-35

Lunch Kit, steel with plastic thermos,
  Aladdin, 1973 65-95

Lunch Kit, soft vinyl with plastic thermos,
  Aladdin, 1974 90-125

Movie Poster, 27 x 41 in., Paramount, 1973 35-50

Record, movie soundtrack with songs by
  Neil Diamond 10-15

Record, book narration by Richard Harris 8-12

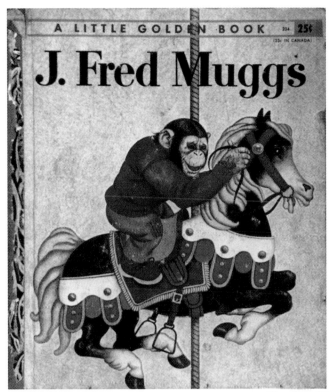

Figure 13-46

Figure 13-47

Figure 13-49

Keiko (*Free Willy*)

Keiko, the killer whale who starred in the original screen hit, *Free Willy*, boasts a life story more thrilling than the film. In a Discovery Channel documentary, "The Free Willy Story: Keiko's Journey Home," Keiko's true story is told.

Keiko was born in the North Atlantic, off the coast of Iceland. Barely two years old in 1979, the whale was trapped in the net of a herring boat, and the ship's captain sold Keiko to Marineland in Ontario, where he joined six other orcas being trained for amusement park work.

After five years in Ontario, Keiko was sold to a zoo in Mexico City for $100,000. He was a big hit, and during the next several years, he grew famous throughout Mexico.

Finally, in 1992, Keiko was cast in the lead role of *Free Willy*. Following the success of the film, Keiko began attracting even more interest—now from people wanting him to be set free in the wild. Warner Brothers helped set up The Free Willy Society, and the zoo agreed to donate Keiko to the cause. But, veterinarians soon realized there was a problem with the plan to free Keiko.

Keiko was sick. Despite excellent care at the hands of his keepers, his pool was too small, and the water in Mexico was too warm. He had developed a skin rash from a virus, which would be contagious to orcas in the wild. Keiko was also suffering from a weakened immune system, and his signature lopped dorsal fin indicated atrophy from lack of exercise.

Undaunted, Keiko's supporters came up with an expensive and complex plan to create a special Whale and Dolphin Rescue Center at an Oregon coast aquarium. Warner Brothers donated $7 million to the project, which needed to be completed in record time in order to have Keiko as its first patient.

Meanwhile, Keiko's condition was worsening. Vets said that, based on blood work, the orca's condition was reaching critical. By the time the rescue center was completed, he could be too sick to survive the long move.

However, ten months later, move day arrived. UPS had donated a plane, and the complicated logistics for lifting the 7,000-pound whale had been carefully figured. Once Keiko had been successfully lifted into a canvas sling and lowered into an ice-laden water tank, he was to be driven to the airport via a secret route at 2 a.m. If he panicked, he would probably die. Despite the late hour, Keiko's transport team was stunned to find the Mexico City streets mobbed with thousands of fans. Keiko's departure erupted into a spontaneous parade, filled with well-wishers who also happened to make Keiko late for his flight.

At the airport, Keiko's plane boarding ordeal also met with snags. If he wasn't in the air before dawn, his water would be too hot before he arrived in Oregon. Finally, at 5 a.m., Keiko was airborne, en route to his new home.

Keiko arrived in Oregon amidst a storm of reporters from around the globe, and thousands and thousands of fans. Yet, incredibly, although he'd spent more than 16 hours in a tight container, Keiko had remained calm and unharmed.

During his months at the Rescue Center, Keiko recovered, his skin rash disappeared, and he grew stronger and stronger. Not only did Keiko's story have a happy ending, the movie spawned a string of sequels.

Mattel issued two Barbie and Keiko toy sets, each with information on the Free Willy-Keiko Foundation. Mattel also notes that they donated $500,000 to the Foundation.

Figure 13-48

Barbie & Keiko Gift Set, Keiko squeaks, squirts
    water, Keiko is 13.5 in. long, Mattel, 1996
    (figure 13-48) $25-35

Book, *Free Willy*, Scholastic paperback with
    color photos, 8 x 8 in., 32 pgs., 1993
    (figure 13-49) 2-4

Book, *Free Willy*, Scholastic paperback novel
    with color photos, 215 pgs., 1993 *(figure 13-50)* . . . 2-4

Book, *Free Willy 2: The Adventure Home*,
    Scholastic paperback novel, photos, 186 pgs.,
    1995 2-4

Fast Food Toys (Long John Silvers)
    Willy (black and white Killer Whale) 4-8

    Jesse (boy) 3-5

Game, "Free Willy Game" 5-10

Life Magazine, cover story, "The Happiest
    Whale in the World," 1996 4-8

Movie Poster, *Free Willy*, one sheet, 27 x 41 in.,
    1993 12-20

Movie Poster, *Free Willy 2*, one sheet, 27 x 41 in.,
    1995 10-15

People Magazine, 1996 2-4

Plush Toy, small size 6-12

Figure 13-50

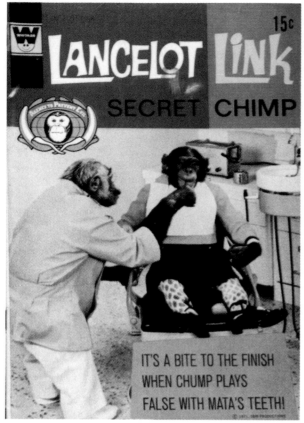

Figure 13-51

Figure 13-52

King (*Sergeant Preston of the Yukon*)

King, Sgt. Preston's faithful husky dog, worked alongside the show's other animal star, Rex, a horse. *Sergeant Preston of the Yukon* aired on CBS from 1955 to 1958. It was conceived by George W. Trendle, who also created *The Lone Ranger* and *The Green Hornet*. The Wrather Corporation produced this show, as well as *Lassie*.

Book, Rand McNally Elf Book, *Sgt. Preston and Yukon King*, #500, 1955 . . . .$10-18

Coloring Book, cover shows King and Sgt. Preston in canoe, Whitman, 1953 20-30

Coloring Book, cover shows King, Rex, and Sgt. Preston, Treasure Books, 1957 20-30

Poster, King and a saluting Sgt. Preston, Quaker premium sent to contest winners, 1950 200-250

Lad, A Dog

Albert Peyson Terhune's classic tale of a valiant collie was committed to the silver screen in 1961, co-starring Angela Cartwright as the young crippled girl who is moved to walk by Lad's courage. The movie also features nice performances by Lady, Lad's "wife," and their puppies, including Wolf and Little Lad.

Comic Book, *Lad, A Dog*, Dell Movie Classic #1303, photo cover, 1961 15-35

Movie Poster, 27 x 41 in., Warner Bros., 1961 . . . 10-15

Lancelot Link, Secret Chimp

The popularity of *James Bond, The Man From U.N.C.L.E.*, and other spy shows was not lost on the animal kingdom. Saturday morning's answer was Lancelot Link, Secret Chimp, a suited and dubbed chimpanzee employed by A.P.E., the Agency to Prevent Evil. The cast of clothed, talking chimps also included Darwin (Lance's boss) and Mata Hairi (his partner). The bad guys, working for C.H.U.M.P., included Wang Fu and Dr. Strangemind.

Lance's band, which performed at the end of each episode, was called Lancelot Link and the Evolution Revolution. The series was introduced in an hour-long format in 1970, and cut to a half hour for its second and final season in 1971-1972.

Comic Book, #1, Gold Key, photo cover,
   April, 1971 . . . .$10-20

Comic Book, #2, Gold Key, photo cover, 1971 8-16

Comic Book, #3-8, Gold Key, 1971-73
   (figure 13-51, 52, 53) 5-10

Lunch Box and Thermos, steel, early 1970s 50-75

Figure 13-53

Leo, the MGM Lion

Leo has one of the best-known cat faces in the country, although several lions have actually filled the role over the years. Leo once guest-starred in a classic *Lassie* episode.

Mug, black ceramic with MGM logo *(figure 13-54)* . . 5-10

Pin-Back Button, photo, "On World Tour,
   The Greatest Star of the Screen," 1930s 15-25

Figure 13-54

Figure 13-55

Marquis Chimps (The Hathaways)

Comic Book, *The Hathaways*, Dell Four Color
#1298, photo cover, 1962 *(figure 13-55)* $10-20

Magazine, *Jack and Jill*, "The Marquis
Chimps," February 1962 3-5

Mister Ed

As thousands of "Ed Heads" will attest, Mister Ed is a collectible classic. Alan Young's brain child, he was a TV favorite for years following his 1961 debut as a syndicated show. CBS quickly picked up *Mister Ed*, and ran the show until September 1966. Alan Young portrayed Wilbur Post, an architect who discovers a horse in his barn, and soon discovers the horse talks—but only to him. Although not credited on the show, former western star Allan "Rocky" Lane, provided the voice of Mister Ed.

Book, *Mr. Ed The Talking Horse*, Little Golden
Book 483, 1962 *(figure 13-56)* 15-20

Book, *The Original Mr. Ed*, by Walter Brooks,
9 stories, Bantam paperback, 1963 15-20

Coloring Book, *Mister Ed*, (shows Ed wearing
sunglasses), Whitman, 1963 40-55

Comic Book, *Mister Ed the Talking Horse*,
Gold Key, #1, Nov. 1962, photo cover
(figure 13-57) 20-90

Comic Book, *Mister Ed the Talking Horse*,
Gold Key, #2-6, photo covers, 1962-64
(figure 13-58) 10-50

Comic Book, *Mister Ed*, Dell Four Color 1295,
early 1960s, Dell Publishing 20-100

Comic Book, March of Comics series #260,
16-page premium, 1964 15-30

Figure 13-57

Game, Mister Ed, box is 9 x 18 in., Parker
Brothers, 1962 .... $70-100

Magazine, *Jack and Jill*, "Mr. Ed—
TV's Talking Horse," November 1962 5-8

Photograph, Nick at Nite promotional 8 x 10 in.
B&W glossy with text at bottom 8-12

Puppet, red and blue cloth body, soft vinyl head,
10 in., Knickerbocker, 1962 50-75

Puppet, *Mister Ed* Talking Puppet, 11.5 in.,
Mattel, 1962 *(figure 13-59)* 75-100

Stool, for TV viewing, stuffed body with vinyl
head and saddle, 1959 175-250

Tote Bag, "Mr. Ed's Feed Bag," Nick at Nite
promotional item, 21 x 16 in., 1990s 50-75

TV Guide, photo cover, "Mister Ed Gets the
Last Laugh," March 31, 1962 35-50

Misty of Chincoteague (and other Chincoteague Ponies)

In the mid-1940s, author Marguerite Henry went to
Chincoteague Island, off the coast of Virginia, and met
Paul and Maureen Beebee. The Beebee's had a pet pony
named Misty, which they had gotten at Pony Penning Day,
an annual summer event on the island since 1925. Ms.
Henry was fascinated with the story of the wild island
ponies and of Pony Penning Day, and decided to write a
book about Misty.

Her book, *Misty of Chincoteague*, is one of the best-loved
horse books of all time, and was made into a film in the
early 1960s. Misty and her foal, Stormy, became celebrities, and made appearances at special events with Ms.
Henry and the Beebees.

Today, Misty and Stormy are stuffed and on display at
the Misty Museum on Assateague.

Figure 13-59

Figure 13-58

Figure 13-56

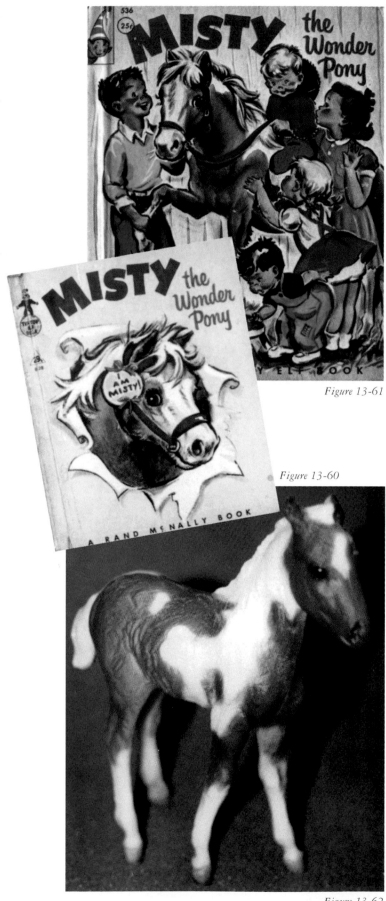

Figure 13-61

Figure 13-60

Figure 13-62

Book, *Misty of Chincoteague, Stormy or Sea Star*, recent hardcover reprint, each $6-12

Book, *Misty the Wonder Pony*, head shot cover, Rand McNally Tip Top Elf Book *(figure 13-60)* 10-15

Book, *Misty the Wonder Pony*, Misty with kids on cover, Rand McNally Tip Top Elf Book *(figure 13-61)* 10-15

Book, *Misty Makes a Movie*, with photos from film, Rand McNally, 1961 10-15

Calendar, Misty of Chincoteague Foundation, Gladstone Media, 1997 10-15

Figure, Misty with trick stool, ceramic, 2 pieces, 3 in., Hagen Renaker, 1990s 65-95

Figure, Misty, painted plastic, 6.75 in., Breyer 25-35

Figure, Stormy as foal, painted plastic, 6 in., Breyer *(figure 13-62)* 20-25

Figure, Sea Star, 5.5 in., Breyer 25-35

Figure, Misty, hollow plastic, 6.25 in., with Pony Penning Day postcard, from Chincoteague 20-25

Figure, Phantom Wings, Misty's foal, painted plastic, 6 in., Breyer 15-25

Playset, Miniature Pony Farm, Chincoteague, VA, 1-in. figures in plastic case with fence 25-30

Stickers, Chincoteague Pony Farm set of 6 puff stickers, Stormy on cart top 10-15

Morris the Cat—9 Lives Cat Food (Star Kist Foods)

Book, *The Morris Approach*, cat care by
Barbara Burn, 1st ed., William & Morrow, 1980
(figure 13-63) $6-10

Cup, Morris picture and name on white mug,
  made by Papél 4-8

Drinking Glass, "There's something irresistible
  about this glass," 9-Lives, no date 8-12

T-Shirt, "Morris for President—1988" with photo
  in center *(figure 13-64)* 10-15

Tote Bag, "Purr if You're a Morris Fan/I'm Morris.
  9-Lives is My Bag," white canvas *(figure 13-65)* . . 12-20

National Velvet (and International Velvet)

National Velvet played alongside a young Elizabeth Taylor
in movie theaters, and with Lori Martin on television.
International Velvet, the 1978 feature film sequel, starred
Tatum O'Neal.

Book, Little Golden Book, *National Velvet*,
  #431, 1961 12-20

Comic Book, *National Velvet*, Gold Key #1 15-40

Comic Book, *National Velvet*, Gold Key #2,
  photo cover, 1963 *(figure 13-66)* 10-25

Lobby Card (with Elizabeth Taylor) 25-45

Lobby Card (without Elizabeth Taylor) 10-20

Figure 13-63

Figure 13-64

Figure 13-65

Figure 13-66

Figure 13-67

Magazine, *Jack and Jill*, "Lori Martin in
National Velvet," August, 1961 . . . . $3-5

Marx Jointed Horse Figure, International Velvet,
1970s 25-40

Movie Poster, *National Velvet*, MGM, 1944
(with Elizabeth Taylor) 175-250

Movie Poster, *International Velvet*, MGM,
1978 (with Tatum O'Neal) 15-25

Paper Dolls, *National Velvet*, Whitman
#1958, early 1960s 40-65

TV Guide, cover, National Velvet, with Lori
Martin, April 8, 1961 *(figure 13-67)* 8-15

Nipper—RCA Victor

Figure, ceramic, GE Comp, made in Sri Lanka,
6.5 in *(figure 13-68)* 20-30

Figure, composition, large size promotional
display, sitting with head tilted
(figure 13-69) 100-175

Pin-Back Button, "Wurlitzer Cincinnati—His
Master's Voice," Gold Medal, 1901 75-100

Pin-Back Button, "Little Nipper Club Member,"
RCA Victor, blue and white, 1940s 15-25

Pin-Back Button, "I'm Voting for RCA Victor—
Bi-Acoustic Radio," yellow, 1930s 15-25

Plush Toy, 22 in., collar with metal plate,
Nipper, Radio Corp. of America 1930s-1940s . . 70-120

Plush Toy, Nipper, 22 in., Dakin, RCA collar,
1993 . . . . $55-85

Plush Toy, Chipper, 12 in., Dakin, RCA collar,
1993 (figure 13-70) 20-35

Salt and Pepper Shakers, figural Nipper, ceramic,
pair (figure 13-71) 20-35

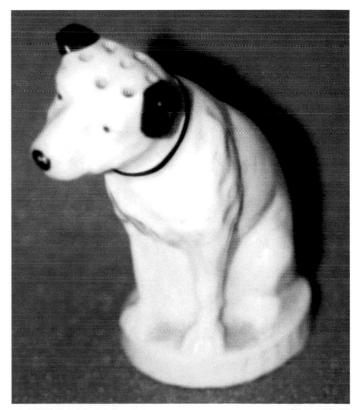

Pete the Pup (*Little Rascals*)

Pete the Pup was a black and white terrier mix with a sig-nature ring painted around one eye. He played a funny street dog in the *Our Gang* movies. His acting specialty was to look scared or guilty by laying down, closing his eyes and putting his paws over his head.

Pin-Back Button, photo, "Member Spanky Safety
Club—Pete," B&W, 1930s 25-50

Figure 13-70

Puzzles, Movie-Land Cut-ups, box holds two
puzzles, 1930s-1940s (figure 13-72) 50-75

Rex (*Sergeant Preston of the Yukon*)

Rex, a horse, co-starred with King, a husky dog in *Sergeant Preston of the Yukon* from 1955 to 1958. (See also listing above for King).

Book, Rand McNally Elf Book, *Sgt. Preston
and Rex*, #569, 1956 10-18

Figure, Rex and Sgt. Preston, black standing horse
& accessories, Hartland Plastics, 1950s 150-300

Figure 13-71

Figure 13-68

Rusty

In the mid-late 1940s, Rusty, a German shepherd, starred in a series of films with Ted Donaldson. Some of Rusty's movies are available on video today.

Movie Posters

The Adventures of Rusty, Columbia, 1945 (Ted Donaldson) $35-50

For the Love of Rusty, Columbia, 1947 (Ted Donaldson) 30-40

Son of Rusty, Columbia, 1947 (Ted Donaldson) 15-25

My Dog Rusty, Columbia, 1948 (Ted Donaldson) 15-25

Rusty Leads the Way, 1948 (Ted Donaldson) 15-25

Rusty Saves a Life, 1948 (Ted Donaldson) 15-25

Rusty's Birthday, 1949 (Ted Donaldson) 15-25

Figure 13-69

Skippy, the Bush Kangaroo

This Australian television series has aired in the U.S. several times. Items relating to the show have been produced in Australia, and are, therefore, tough to find in the States.

Book, Little Golden Book, *Skippy the Bush Kangaroo*, #379 20-35

Book, Little Golden Book, *Skippy to the Rescue* 20-35

Strongheart

The first dramatic dog star, this German shepherd paved the way for Rin Tin Tin to shoot to stardom in the early 1920s. Strongheart's big break came in the 1921 film, *The Silent Call*. He also starred in *Brawn of the North*, *The Love Master*, and the earliest film version of Jack London's *White Fang*. Today, he is immortalized on cans of Strongheart dog food.

Book, *Letters to Strongheart*, by J. Allen Boone,
   1920s $25-40

Book, *Strongheart, the Story of a Wonder Dog*,
   Whitman, 1926 40-65

Dog Food, Strongheart, full can
   (liver or beef flavor!) . . . . 50¢-75¢

Movie Poster, *The Silent Call*, 1921 150-250

Figure 13-72

Tamba the Talented Chimp

Tamba starred with Johnny Weissmuller in his *Jungle Jim* film series.

Lobby Card, *Killer Ape*, Columbia Pictures,
   1953 (scene dependent) (*figure 13-73*) 10-15

Figure 13-73

Toto

Let's face it. Without Toto, there would be no *Wizard of Oz*. Really—no mean Mrs. Gulch, upset that Toto bit her, no need for Dorothy to run away, no one to break free of the witch's castle to get help for Dorothy, and no one to pull the curtain away at the end, exposing the wizard's true identity.

Toto made that film. He was ably portrayed by a Cairn terrier named Terry, trained under the patient tutelage of Carl Spitz.

Figure 13-74

Lobby Card, *The Wizard of Oz*, 1939 (scene
dependent) $200-350

Musical Plate, "Over the Rainbow," Knowles
(figure 13-74) 20-35

Promotional Photo, B&W, 8 x 10 in., Judy
Garland and Terry as Toto 4-8

Vance The Talking Pig
When *Big Top Pee Wee* premiered in 1988, Pee Wee had a
fabulous new sidekick—his talking pet pig, Vance.

Book, *Big Top Pee Wee*, soft cover picture book,
1988 10-18

Talking Plush Toy, 10 x 16 in., Matchbox,
1988 *(figure 13-75)* 45-60

White Fury
White Fury, dubbed "King of the Wild Horses," starred in
a 1930s Nat Levine serial called *The Golden Stallion*.

Pin-Back Button, text and B&W graphic of
fighting horses, 1930s 10-15

Willy (*Free Willy*—see Keiko)

Yukon King (*Sergeant Preston of the Yukon*—see King)

Zeus and Roxanne

Zeus and Roxanne, released in 1997, tells the story of a unique friendship that develops between a dog and a dolphin.

Prop, dog dish used on the set of the film,
    gray plastic $20-35

Miscellaneous and Group Shots

Book, *Beauty of the Beasts—Tales of Hollywood's Wild Animal Stars*, by Ralph Helfer, 1990 10-15

Book, *Dog Stars of Hollywood*, 5 x 4.5 in.,
    Saalfield #1594, photos throughout, 1936 40-65

Book, *Not So Dumb—Animals in the Movies*,
    by Raymond Lee, Castle Books, 1970 7-12

Book, *Performing Dogs*, by Elizabeth Ring,
    children's hardcover, Millbrook Press, 1994 5-10

Figure 13-75

The Patsy Award Winners

Between 1951 and 1986, the American Humane Association gave out awards for outstanding animal performers. Known as the "Patsy Awards," the prizes were given to animals working in film, television, stage, and commercials.

1951

First Place: Francis, a mule, *Francis the Talking Mule* (U.I.)

Second Place: California, a horse, *The Palomino* (Columbia)

Third Place: Pierre, a chimp, *My Friend Irma Goes West* (Paramount)

Craven Award: Jerry Brown, a falling horse (Ace Hudkins, owner and trainer)

Awards of Excellence:

- Flame, a dog, *My Pal* series (RKO)
- Lassie, a collie, *Challenge of Lassie* (MGM)
- Black Diamond, a horse, *Black Midnight*, (Lindsay Parsons-Monogram)
- Jackie, a lion, *Samson and Delilah* (Paramount)

1952

First Place: Rhubarb, a cat, *Rhubarb* (Paramount)

Second Place: Francis, a mule, *Francis Goes to the Races* (U.I.)

Craven Award: Smoky, a fighting stallion (Fat Jones, owner and trainer)

Awards of Excellence:

- Chinook, a dog, *Yukon Manhunt* (Monogram)
- Diamond, a horse, *Flame of Araby* (U.I.)
- Corky, a dog, *Behave Yourself* (Wald-Krasna-RKO)

1953

First Place: Jackie, a lion, *Fearless Fagan* (MGM)

Second Place: Bonzo, a chimp, *Bonzo Goes to College* (U.I.)

Third Place: Trigger, a horse, *Son of Paleface* (Paramount)

Craven Award: Bracket, a jumping horse (Hudkins Stables, owner)

Awards of Excellence:

- Francis, a mule, *Francis Goes to West Point* (U.I.)
- Tramp, Jr., a dog, *Room for One More* (Warner Bros.)
- Cheta, a chimp, *Tarzan's Savage Fury* (Sol Lesser)
- Chinook, a dog, *Yukon Gold* (Wm. F. Broidy Productions)

1954

First Place: Sam, a dog, *Hondo* (Wayne-Fellows Prod.)

Second Place: Francis, a mule, *Francis Covers the Big Town* (U.I.)

Third Place: Jackie, a lion, *Androcles and the Lion* (RKO)

Craven Award: Cocaine, a falling horse (Chuck Roberson, owner and trainer)

Awards of Excellence:

- Baron, a dog, *Back to God's Country* (U.I.)
- Peggy, a chimp, *Valley of the Headhunters* (Columbia)
- Jackie, a lion, *White Witch Doctor* (Fox)

1955

First Place: Gypsy, a horse, *Gypsy Colt* (MGM)

Second Place: Francis, a mule, *Francis Joins the WACS* (U.I.)

Third Place: Esmeralda, a seal, *20,000 Leagues Under the Sea* (Walt Disney Productions)

Craven Award: Flash, a falling and lay-down horse (Henry Willis, owner and trainer)

Awards of Excellence:

- Shep, a dog, *A Bullet is Waiting* (Howard Welsch Prod.)
- Satin, a tiger, *Demetrius and the Gladiator* (Fox)
- Outlaw, a horse, *Black Horse Canyon* (U.I.)
- Beauty, a horse, *Outlaw Stallion* (Columbia)

1956

First Place Wildfire, a dog, *It's a Dog's Life* (MGM)

Second Place: Francis, a mule, *Francis Joins the Navy* (U.I.)

Third Place: Faro, a dog, *The Kentuckian*, (Hecht-Lancaster Prod.)

Craven Award: Flame, a dog (Frank Barnes, owner and trainer)

1957

First Place: Samantha, a goose, *Friendly Persuasion* (Allied Artists)

Second Place: War Winds, a horse, *Giant* (Warner Bros.)

Third Place: Francis, a mule, *Francis in the Haunted House* (U.I.)

Craven Award: King Cotton, a horse (Ralph McCutcheon, owner and trainer)

Awards of Excellence:

- Silver, a horse, *The Lone Ranger* (Warner Bros.)
- Lady, a dog, *Goodbye, My Lady* (Batjac Prods.)
- Bascom, a dog, *Hollywood or Bust* (Paramount)

1958

Motion Pictures

First Place: Spike, a dog, *Old Yeller* (Walt Disney Prods.)

Second Place: Beauty, a horse, *Wild is the Wind* (Paramount)

Third Place: Kelly, a dog, *Kelly and Me* (U.I.)

Awards of Excellence:

- Tony, a horse, *Hoofs and Goofs* short subject

Television

First Place: Lassie, a dog, *Lassie* series (Jack Wrather Prods.)

Second Place: Cleo, a dog, *The People's Choice* (Norden Prods.)

Third Place: Rin Tin Tin, a dog, *Adventures of Rin Tin Tin* (Herbert B. Leonard Prods.)

Craven Award: Trigger, a horse (Roy Rogers, owner, and Glen Randall, trainer)

Awards of Excellence:

- Flicka, a horse, *My Friend, Flicka* (Fox TV)

1959

Motion Pictures

First Place: Pyewacket, a cat, *Bell, Book and Candle* (Columbia)

Second Place: Tonka, a horse, *Tonka* (Walt Disney Productions)

Third Place: Henry, a rabbit, *The Geisha Boy* (Paramount)

Awards of Excellence:

- King, a dog, *The Proud Rebel* (Formosa Prods.)

Television

First Place: Lassie, a dog, *Lassie* series (Jack Wrather Prods.)

Second Place: Asta, a dog, *The Thin Man* (MGM TV)

Third Place: Rin Tin Tin, a dog, *Adventures of Rin Tin Tin* (Screen Gems)

Craven Award: Baldy, a rearing horse, Fat Jones Stables, owner, and William "Buster" Trow, trainer

Awards of Excellence:

- Jasper, a dog, *Bachelor Father* (Bachelor Prods.)

1960

Motion Pictures

First Place: Shaggy, a dog, *The Shaggy Dog* (Walt Disney Prods.)

Second Place: Herman, a pigeon, *The Gazebo* (MGM)

Third Place: North Wind, a horse, *The Sad Horse* (Fox)

Television

First Place: Asta, a dog, *The Thin Man* (MGM TV)

Second Place: Lassie, a dog, *Lassie* series (Jack Wrather Prods.)

Third Place: Fury, a horse, *Fury* series (TPA Prods.) and Jasper, a dog, *Bachelor Father* (Bachelor Prods)—tie

Craven Award: Sharkey, Dempsey, Choctaw and Joker, a four-up team of horses (Hudkins Bros. Stables, owner)

1961

Motion Pictures

First Place: King Cotton, a horse, *Pepe* (Columbia)

Second Place: Spike, a dog, *Dog of Flanders* (Fox)

Third Place: Mr. Stubbs, a chimp, *Toby Tyler* (Walt Disney) and Skip, a dog, *Visit to a Small Planet*, (Hal Wallis Prods.)—tie

Television

First Place: Tramp, a dog, *My Three Sons* (Don Federson Prods.)

Second Place: Lassie, a dog, *Lassie* series (Jack Wrather Prods.)

Third Place: Fury, a horse, *Fury* series (Jack Wrather Prods.)

1962

Motion Pictures

First Place: Cat, *Breakfast at Tiffany's* (Paramount)

Second Place: Pete, a dog, *The Silent Call* (Fox)

Third Place: Flame, a horse, *The Clown and the Kid* (United Artists)

Television

First Place: Mr. Ed, a horse, *Mr. Ed* series (Mister Ed Company)

Second Place: Lassie, a dog, *Lassie* series (Jack Wrather Prods.)

Third Place: Tramp, a dog, *My Three Sons* (Don Federson Prod.)

1963

Motion Pictures

First Place: Big Red, a dog, *Big Red* (Walt Disney Prods.)

Second Place: Sydney, an elephant, *Jumbo* (MGM)

Third Place: Zamba, a lion, *The Lion* (Fox)

Television

First Place: Mr. Ed, a horse, *Mr. Ed* series (Mister Ed Company)

Second Place: Lassie, a dog, *Lassie* series (Jack Wrather Prods.)

Third Place: Tramp, a dog, *My Three Sons* (Don Federson Prods.)

Craven Award: Mickey O'Boyle, trained "fighting" horse

1964

Motion Pictures

First Place: Tom Dooley, a dog, *Savage Sam* (Walt Disney Prods.)

Second Place: Pluto, a dog, *My Six Loves* (Paramount)

Third Place: Raunchy, a jaguar, *Rampage* (Warner Bros.)

Television

First Place: Lassie, a dog, *Lassie* series (Jack Wrather Prods.)

Second Place: Mr. Ed, a horse, *Mr. Ed* series (Mister Ed Company)

Third Place: Tramp, a dog, *My Three Sons* (Don Federson Prods.)

1965

Motion Pictures

First Place: Patrina, a tiger, *A Tiger Walks* (Walt Disney Prods.)

Second Place: Storm, a dog, *Goodbye Charlie* (Fox)

Third Place: Junior, a dog, *Island of the Blue Dolphins* (Radnitz-Universal)

Television

First Place: Flipper, a dolphin, *Flipper* series (Tors-MGM)

Second Place: Lassie, a dog, *Lassie* series (Jack Wrather Prods.)

Third Place: Mr. Ed, a horse, *Mr. Ed* series (Filmways)

Craven Award: Lucky Buck, a trained "lay down" horse

1966

Motion Pictures

First Place: Syn Cat, a cat, *That Darn Cat* (Walt Disney Prods.)

Second Place: Clarence, a lion, *Clarence the Cross-Eyed Lion* (Tors-MGM)

Third Place: Judy, a chimp, *Merlin Jones* (Walt Disney Prods.)

Television

First Place: Flipper, a dolphin, *Flipper* series (Tors-MGM)

Second Place: Lord Nelson, a dog, *Please Don't Eat the Daisies* (MGM)

Third Place: Higgins (Benji), a dog, *Petticoat Junction* (Filmways)

Craven Award: Smokey, a trick horse

1967

Motion Pictures

First Place: Elsa, a lion, *Born Free* (Columbia)

Second Place: Duke, a dog, *The Ugly Dachshund* (Walt Disney Prods.)

Third Place: Vindicator, a bull, *The Rare Breed* (Universal)

Television

First Place: Judy, a chimp, *Daktari* (Tors-MGM)

Second Place: Flipper, a dolphin, *Flipper* series (Tors-MGM)

Third Place: Arnold, a pig, *Green Acres* (Filmways)

1968

Motion Pictures

First Place: Ben, a bear, *Gentle Giant* (Paramount-Ivan Tors)

Second Place: Sir Tom, a cougar, *The Cat* (Cine-Cal Prods.)

Third Place: Sophie, a sea lion, *Doctor Doolittle* (Fox)

Television

First Place: Arnold, a pig, *Green Acres* (Filmways)

Second Place: Ben, a bear, *Gentle Ben* (Ivan Tors)

Third Place: Clarence, a lion, *Daktari* (Tors-MGM)

TV Commercial Award: Zamba, a lion, for Dreyfus Fund

1969

Motion Pictures

First Place: Albarado, a horse, *The Man in the Gray Flannel Suit* (Walt Disney Prods.)

Television

First Place: Arnold, a pig, *Green Acres* (Filmways)

Second Place: Timmy, a chimp, *The Beverly Hillbillies* (single performance) (Filmways)

TV Commercial Award: Chauncey, a cougar, for Ford Motor Company

1970

Motion Pictures: Rascal, a raccoon, *Rascal* (Walt Disney Prods.)

Television—series: Scruffy, a dog, *The Ghost and Mrs. Muir* (Fox)

Television—non-series: Algae, a seal for a single performance in *The Ghost and Mrs. Muir* (Fox)

Craven Award: Kilroy, a falling horse

1971

Motion Pictures: Sancho, a wolf, *The Wild Country* (Walt Disney Prods.)

Television—series: Arnold, a pig, *Green Acres* (Filmways)

Television—non-series: Margie, an elephant, *The Boy Who Stole an Elephant* (Walt Disney Prods.) and Lassie's pups, *Lassie* (Jack Wrather)

1972

Motion Pictures: Ben, a rat, *Willard* (Bing Crosby Prods.)

Television—series: Pax, a dog, *Longstreet* (Paramount)

Television—non-series: Ott, a horse, *Lassie* (Jack Wrather Prods.)

Craven Award: Cocaine, a horse, for outstanding stunt work

1973

Motion Pictures: Ben, a rat, *Ben* (Bing Crosby Prods.)

Television—series: Farouk, a dog, *Ironside* (Universal TV)

Television—non-series: Ott, a horse, *Bonanza*, single performance (NBC TV)

Special Commercial Award: Morris, a cat, for Nine Lives Cat Food

Hall of Fame: Lassie

1974

Motion Pictures: Alpha, a dolphin, *Day of the Dolphin* (Avco-Embassy)

Television—series: Midnight, a cat, *Mannix* (Paramount TV)

Television—non-series: Caesar, a dog, *Trapped* (Universal TV)

Special Commercial Award: Scruffy, a dog, for Chuck Wagon Dog Food

1975

Motion Pictures: Tonto, a cat, *Harry and Tonto* (Fox)

Television—series: Elsa, a lion, *Born Free* (NBC TV)

Television—non-series: Ginger and pups, a coyote family, *The Indestructible Outcasts* (NBC TV)

Special Commercial Award: Lawrence, a red deer, for Hartford Insurance

Hall of Fame: Benji

1976

Grand Patsy Award: Fred, A cockatoo, *Baretta* (Universal TV)

Category I—Wild Animals: Billie, a chimp, *Swiss Family Robinson* (Fox)

Category II—Canine: Tiger, a dog, *A Boy and His Dog* (L.Q. Jones Prods.)

Category III—Equine: Ott, a horse, *Run, Joe, Run* (D'Angelo Prods.)

Category IV—Special: Fred, a cockatoo, *Baretta* (Universal TV)

1977

Grand Patsy Award: Fred, A cockatoo, *Baretta* (Universal TV)

Category I—Wild Animals: Neal, a lion, *The Bionic Woman* (Universal TV)

  Heller, a cougar, *Shazam* (Filmation)

  Lawrence, a red deer, Hartford Insurance ad

  Snoopy, a raccoon, *Guardian of the Wilderness* (Schick-Sunn Classic)

  Bruno, a bear, *Wilderness Family* (Pacific International Enterprises)

  Valentine, a camel, *Hawmps* (Mulberry Square Prods.)

Category II—Canine: Gus, a dog, *Won Ton Ton* (Paramount)

  Five Doberman dogs, *The Amazing Dobermans*, (Rosamond)

  Bourbon, a dog, *Call of the Wild* (Charles Fried Prods.)

  Kodiac and sled team, dogs, *Call of the Wild* (Charles Fried Prods.)

Category III—Equine: Shoshone, a horse, *Mustang Country* (Universal)

  Yoyo, a horse, *Banjo Hackett* (Columbia)

  Yoyo, a horse, *Shaggy D.A.* (Walt Disney Prods.)

  Gus, a mule, *Gus* (Walt Disney Prods.)

  unnamed horse, *Top Choice Dog Food* ad

Category IV—Special: 17, a cat, *Dr. Shrinker* (Sid and Marty Krofft)

  Jojo, a raven, *Duffy Moon* (Daniel Wilson Prods.)

  Fred, a cockatoo, *Baretta* (Universal TV)

Hall of Fame: Scruffy, a dog, *The Ghost and Mrs. Muir*

1978

Category I—Wild Animals: Farkas, a wolf, *Lucan* (MGM TV)

Category II—Canine: Sam, a yellow Labrador Retriever, *Sam* (Mark VII Ltd.)

Category III—Equine: Domengo, a horse, *Peter Lundy and the Medicine Hat Stallion* (Ed Friendly Prods.)

Category IV—Special: Amber, a cat, *The Cat from Outer Space* (Walt Disney Prods.)

Craven Award: Sandy, a dog, from the Broadway production *Annie*

Special Service Award: Betty White

1979 - 1982

No awards presented

1983

Category I—Wild Animals: C.J., an orangutan, *The Fall Guy* (20th Century Fox)

Category II—Canine: Boomer, a mutt, *Here's Boomer* (Paramount)

Category III—Equine: Kit Kat, a horse, *The Fall Guy* (20th Century Fox)

Category IV—Special: Jeckel, a bull, *Knight Rider* (Universal TV)

American Human/Kal Kan/Animal Bond Award: O.J., a mutt owned and trained by Bob Weatherwax, from *Skeezer* (ITC Entertainment)

1984

Wild Animal Category: Black leopards, *Manimal* (20th Century Fox)

Canine Category: Tundra, *Love Boat* (Aaron Spelling Prods.)

Special Category: Merlin, a hawk, *Manimal* (20th Century Fox)

Hall of Fame: Neal, a lion, owned and trained by Ron Oxley

   Harry, a black Labrador/Great Dane mix owned and trained by Karl Lewis Miller

Human/Animal Bond Award: Am, a seal, *The Gold Seal* (Samuel Goldwyn Jr. Prods.)

1985

Wild Animal Category: J.R., an orangutan, *Goin' Bananas* (Hanna-Barbera)

Canine Category: Folsom, *Body Double* (Columbia)

Equine Category: Silver, a horse, *The Yellow Rose* (Warner Bros.)

Human/Animal Bond Award: Sneakers, a puppy, *Highway to Heaven* (Michael Landon Prods.)

1986

Wild Animal Category: Dee, a chimp, *Simon and Simon* (Universal)

Canine Category: Samson, Magnum and Lucan, Doberman Pinschers, *Remo Williams: The Adventure Begins* (Orion)

Equine Category: Tis No Trouble, a horse, *Sylvester* (Rastar/Columbia)

Special Category: The cats, *Alfred Hitchcock Presents* (Universal)

1987 - present

No awards presented